SEO

Marketing Strategies to Dominate the First Page

Grant Kennedy

that the author is not engaging in the rendering of legal, financial, medical or professional advice.

Contents list

Page

Introduction

You have picked up this book because you saw the words 'SEO', and you immediately realized that this is the buzz term in order to send much-needed traffic towards your website and business.

Well done! This is a smart move on your part!

Throughout this book we will discuss in detail exactly what SEO is, and we will talk about strategies which help drive that traffic in your direction. Some of these strategies and terms may seem complicated and confusing at first, however it's important to say that you should certainly read to the end, because it will all become very clear indeed!

If you have no idea what SEO is, or how to use it, then you have come to the right place, as we will certainly leave you in no doubt by the end of this book about the sheer importance of this initiative.

Traffic = custom, and we know that custom = money!

Okay, so first things first.

We know that it is certainly one thing starting your own business and building a quality website, but it's quite another thing to get that website working for you, in order to bring the customers flooding in. You could easily spend thousands on the right site but find that it all falls flat on its face if you don't get the ground work done effectively in the first place – this is where SEO comes in.

Search engine optimization, or SEO for short, is the only way to make sure your website is visible to everyone, and the only way to bring in the results that you need. Done right, SEO will improve your rankings hand over fist, it will drive traffic to your site in volumes you may never have dreamed of, and it will make you visible in search engine top search pages. If you can get SEO right, your website will always be on page one of search engine pages, and that means a significant leap in visitors to your website.

SEO isn't just about having a website that is search engine friendly however, it is about making your site friendly to your visitors, friendly enough to convert them into paying customers. The biggest search engines in the world, like Google, Yahoo! and Bing, will drive most of the traffic to your site; whilst the social media sites will drive a certain amount, it is the search engines that you need to be playing to.

Search engines are unique. They will send you traffic that is targeted, i.e. people who are looking for exactly what you are providing. If a search engine does not see your website, then no one else will either and you are missing out on some of the most incredible opportunities there are to make money.

So why can't the search engine find you on its own?

While a search engine is smart, it still needs a little help. Search engines crawl the web, looking for results for their users but there is a limit to how much they can do. If your SEO is done wrong or not at all, your website will be buried so deep that no one will find it; done right, it will bring you in thousands upon thousands of visitors.

Look at it this way, how many websites are on the Internet? Far too many to count, so you need to do some serious work into getting your particular site visible, in order to reach customers, and keep the ones you already have. SEO will help you do that, and it will keep you at the top of the ranking, provided you do it right, provided you pay it the quality and high attention level it deserves.

You can easily do your own SEO, provided you do the research, in order to understand and know how it's done properly. What I am going to tell you within this book is how you can get your website to dominate the first page of the search engines; I will tell you how a search engine works, what you should and shouldn't be doing, and the top tips for getting your website to the number one spot. I will also tell you about pitfalls, and the scams you should avoid at all costs.

Across this book, I will be providing you with information on how to tie your content marketing strategy to your SEO strategy, and how to include social media to your list of marketing strategies too. On top of this, I will be giving you an overview of some of the best tools available for you to measure the true success of your SEO marketing strategy, such as Google Analytics and Google Webmaster. These are two of the most important tools you can have in terms of pushing your website to the top of the search engine rankings, and as we have mentioned countless times already in the short introduction to this book – being at the top of the search rankings is a fast track to money in your bank account.

So, if you are ready to make money, and if you're not, why are you even in this business, let's get started on the journey to SEO heaven.

Chapter 1

What is SEO and How Does it Work?

SEO might seem like a deep and mysterious thing but, really, in reality, it isn't. As with anything in life, everything seems confusing and almost impossible, until you understand it in its entirety, and once you do, the mystery is solved!

SEO isn't rocket science and it certainly isn't brain surgery but, believe it or not, in terms of your business, it is just as important. You won't be required to undertake anything particular complicated once you understand the mechanics of SEO, but learning how to do it takes time and effort; these are two things you should certainly be prepared to invest above everything else.

So, what is SEO and how do these search engines, that we take for granted, actually work?

SEO is an acronym for Search Engine Optimization, and it does exactly what it says on the tin. SEO is all about optimizing your website, and your overall content, so that the search engines can find it easily. SEO is all about ranking in the search engines, and basically about putting your website at the top. If your name comes up on page 1 of the search engine results, traffic to your website will increase significantly – think about it, when you're browsing the web, do you look past page 1, or very rarely page 2, when you search for something on Google? Probably not!

Nobody wants to be trawling through endless pages of results, because quite frankly, we know that the best is always at the top. Now, whilst that mindset might be correct, it could also be that your website is much more quality in terms of content, but if you don't get your marketing and indeed your SEO correct, you will be hidden amongst much more mediocre results. Not fair? Definitely not, but this is the reality of the situation.

Because of this, we all know that, given the right website, and the right marketing, traffic can be converted to sales quite easily.

To truly understand how SEO works, we need to understand how the search engines work. To make it easy to digest, basically, a search engine trawls all the content on the internet, all the websites, the articles, videos, even adverts, looking for specific information; it wants to see certain things on your webpages (known as onsite SEO) or information about your website elsewhere (known as offsite SEO). A search engine is working on behalf of the searcher, to avoid mediocre results cropping up – basically, the search engine is aiming to give the person doing the search the best for their time, and how a search engine works is actually quite complicated.

When it finds the information, a search engine will then use certain formulas to make an analysis of all the information and data it has gleaned. Search engines do this to work out which websites they should show when a person makes a search on the engine by typing in specific keyword phrases; they also work out which order the pages should be shown in. As we mentioned, understanding how a search engine works in a technical manner is difficult, because they are highly specialized beasts, however what you do need to understand is that in order to make the most of your marketing strategies, you need to make the search engine happy.

How SEO Works

Search engines never stop working; they never stop searching and are constantly refining the way that they rank individual webpages. However, there are two elements that are absolutely vital to ranking on page 1 of those search results:

Onsite SEO

Onsite SEO is all about your website, the way it is structured and the content on it. If you want to be on the first page, this has to be top notch. Onsite SEO is all about:

- Targeting the top, most relevant keyword clusters

- Matching existing content so that it targets specific clusters of keywords

- Coming up with new content to target specific clusters

- Having a top notch infrastructure on your website

We will discuss a little later in this book about the more in-depth ways to create a top quality website, because if you don't have quality to market, then really, what is the point?

Offsite SEO

Offsite SEO is about how your website and content is referenced in other places online. For offsite SEO to be successful, you must:

- Develop a high quality profile that revolves around incoming links

- Be active on social media, with relevant high quality content

- Create some non-linking citations about you

- Ensure that at least 50% of your SEO outcome is fully influenced by external sources, which are not in your direct control

Everything else comes down to tactics, strategy and techniques, as well as a certain amount of finesse. Whether you decide to do your SEO yourself, or you hire someone else to take over the mantel for you, understanding what needs to be done is imperative, in order to have a well-rounded view of what needs to happen.

A search engine looks at more than 200 different signals when it evaluates each web page, and it does all this in a matter of seconds; clever, I think you'll agree. Each year, at least another 400 refinements are added, so the most challenging part of SEO is keeping up to date with those signals and refinements – if you don't, your website will sink without a trace. An SEO professional will be able to do this on your behalf, which certainly takes plentiful stress away from your hands, but if you don't have the cash to pay someone else to do the honors, it's important to stay abreast of these developments.

How important are keywords?

SEO is all about keywords, so these are the most important things to consider when building your website, writing content, and adding your Meta descriptions.

As a side note, if you don't know what a Meta description is, let's give you a brief rundown; put simply, a Meta description is a short opening gambit which describes your content and is shown on the search engine results.

When you search for something, perhaps you search for the word 'apple', then the results which come up will have the name and link first, and then underneath there will be a very brief description of what you can expect from the link you're about to click on – this is the Meta description, so it is important to have the keyword present in this description, whilst also being attention-grabbing and eye-catching. Basically, you want to whet the reader's appetite, and make them want to click, in order to read more.

When a person types a search term into a search engine, about 25% of those terms will be ones that the search engine has never heard of before - this is where keyword clusters enter the fray, and this is where you need to take advantage of that gap in the searching adventure.

Keyword clusters are groups of keywords and keyword phrases which focus on high volume core phrases; an example of this would a core phrase of "accommodation". The keyword cluster might include words like "accommodation New York", and "luxury accommodation". We will talk in more detail later on about AdWords, but this is where you can find out the best combinations in order to grab the most traffic; phrases might not come to your mind from guess work, so knowing exactly what you need to target is imperative.

The key to using keywords in SEO is to find the right balance in the targeted keyword phrase list - the balance that delivers you the best return on your investment (ROI). If you can get this right, then you have made a major leap forward.

Matching keywords with existing and new content

One of the best approaches to onsite SEO is to match up a single keyword phrase from each of your clusters to a specific page on your website.

Your home page should be focused on your main keyword phrase, and the navigation pages will each focus on the next important keyword phrases. The least important page on your website will have the least important keyword, but it must still be a keyword that comes up in the search terms, and all the keyword phrases need to be used.

Very often, you will find that none of your webpages are relevant to a keyword phrase that you specifically want to target; in this case, you would need to look at creating a new page centered around that phrase, to take advantage of that gap in your content and keyword opportunities.

Offsite SEO – Your link profile

When it comes to offsite SEO, it is very simple; when a search engine sees an external link to your website, from another online source – this is seen as a big thumbs up, and a vote of confidence for your website. A search engine believes that, if another website is linking to yours then you have a good website to link to in the first place, and that will increase your rankings. However, before you go buying links back to your site, bear in mind that things have evolved significantly.

These days, a search engine will not just take the number of links into account when they are evaluating your profile; in fact, if they see too many links, they can downgrade your ranking. They will look at:

- The trust or reputation value of each site linking to yours

- The relevance or the theme of the sites linking to yours

- The "anchor text" used in the links to your website. The anchor text is the wording used to embed the link.

It is for this reason that you can't simply find a friend who is running a website and constantly do each other a favor by linking back to each other's' sites – the search engine will pick up on this and you may be downgraded because of it.

Offsite SEO – Your social media profile

Where social media sites used to be pretty much ignored by the search engines, they are now one of the biggest references to your business, and the search engines are sitting up and taking note. A little later in this book we will talk about the importance of social media a little more, as well as providing a few hints and tip on how to make use of them, with a tie-in link on your main website. If you ignore social media, you are missing out in a big, big way.

Social media references are providing the search engines with very important signals, signals that reference how good your website is, as well as how successful your overall business is too. It isn't just about opening up a Facebook account however, it's more about having a business page, about being active, and about sharing relevant and quality content, as well as how your associates refer to your website, to you and to your company.

This is a subject for another book however!

Offsite SEO – Your citation profile

A citation is a non-linking reference to you, to your company, your website, or even your phone number. These references will not actually link to you, but the search engine will recognize them. All references to your company are good, but citations are very useful in terms of search results.

This chapter explains in a nutshell what SEO is, and how it works; the rest is all down to strategy, to the techniques that you use, as well as your tactics and finesse.

If you have read this far and you are a little puzzled, let's now break it down into bite-sized chunks. This is not about going over old ground, but rather reiterating just how important SEO is, and giving it the time and attention it deserves. If you understand something, you have the power to exploit it to your advantage, to the max.

An easy definition of SEO

It's all very well and good us sat here talking about SEO like we actually know what it is and what it entails, but if you only have a loose grip on what it means, you're not really going to understand much of this book in its entirety! As we just mentioned at the end of our last section, understanding is key.

Let's take a step backwards for a second and truly define exactly what SEO is, just to re-jog your memory and imprint the whole process on your brain.

As a definition, SEO is:

"Search Engine Optimization (SEO) is the process of affecting the visibility of a website or a web page in a web search engine's unpaid results – often referred to as "natural", "organic", or "earned" results"

Wikipedia puts it very well, I think you'll agree!

This is basically what SEO is – it is essentially manipulating the Internet to a degree, in order to benefit your particular business. Websites can be optimized in order to bring traffic in your direction, and traffic much of the time equates to sales. Of course, on a very basic note, sales mean money for you, and that is what business is all about at the end of the day.

SEO is achieved through many different aims, but one of the main aspect is down to keywords. We will discuss the importance of keywords and how to choose the best possible ones in more detail throughout this book, having mentioned it very briefly in this chapter, but it is important to note that SEO is not all about the careful choice of words. Any SEO professional worth his or her salt will be able to come up with a strategy that is about much more than keywords, and this includes knowing exactly how your website is performing in terms of traffic, clicks, and links back, as well as identifying problem areas and working them out, in order to improve the situation.

Put simply, SEO is a complicated subject, and a subject that has many different corners to try and work out. Yes, you can do it yourself, as we have mentioned countless times, but you will need to read and train yourself in every single facet of the subject before jumping in. There are countless professionals who will offer you their services for a fee, and perhaps it is better to go down this route, and take advantage of their much more advanced skills, provided you choose the correct individual in the first place, of course. Again, we will discuss what you need to look for when hiring a professional, a little later in this book.

Why is SEO important?
Surely, it's obvious, isn't it? SEO brings traffic to your website, and a large percentage of that traffic will buy a product or service from you; even if they don't buy anything, they may give word of mouth referral to another person, and they may buy something.

The Internet has opened up the world for businesses, and that means countless thousands, if not millions, more prospective customers. Working out the best possible way to reach these people, and put your products and services forward is money very well spent indeed, and SEO is one of the major driving forces towards that extra traffic, and extra revenue for your business.

Does it make sense now?
You could be forgiven for feeling a little confused by all this talk of optimization and using search engines, but the bottom line of SEO is not that confusing; it's generally the actual ways and methods of doing it that cause the most puzzled expressions.

Think of it simply and use the words in the phrase – optimize your traffic, and optimize your sales. It's really that simple.

Chapter 2

How Does a Search Engine Really Work? PPC vs Organic SEO

The very first step to being able to optimize your online SEO campaign is to understand that search engines work very differently with paid searches and organic searches.

Having a solid understanding of how a search engine actually works is key to understanding how SEO works, as well as how to increase your rankings on the Search Engine Results Page (SERP); this is the page that comes up when a person types a search query into a search engine. Put simply, the first page they see is where you want to be. If you are a little confused by these different types of search results, don't worry, because I will discuss them in more simplistic terms very shortly, to reiterate understanding.

SERPs are divided up into two types of results – organic, or natural SEO, and the paid search results. The paid search results are typically to the side of the page and these are ads which the search engine perceives to be relevant to the search query.

So, how does it all work?

Organic or Natural SEO

All day long, search engines are sending out crawlers, programs called "spiders". When a search engine finds a website, they send spiders out to follow all the links in that website, and they do this every second of every day. As we mentioned in our previous chapter, understanding the technical side of how a search engine works is very difficult, but generally speaking, you only need a brief overview, in order to get the grasp that you need.

A spider can only follow links that move from one page to another page, and one site to another site; this is why inbound links, those that link from an eternal source to your website, are so important. Basically, these links give the spiders something to chew on and to follow.

When a spider locates a page, it indexes that page, storing the information on the search engine servers. When a person runs a search on that search engine, they are not searching the internet, and instead they are searching the servers of the specific search engine they are using, based on the information that the spiders have found and indexed. It is for this reason that you need to make sure you are giving the spiders what they want and what they are looking for, so they index your site and your content, in order to bring it up in searches that are undertaken by your prospective audience, and hopefully those who turn out to be customers making sales.

It sounds complicated at first, but it's really not!

The search engine will throw up a list of results, a list that is in order of ranking and provided by the algorithm that the search engine uses. This algorithm is a piece of software which works to calculate the value of a page, using a number of factors. These factors include the relevance of the page to the actual search query that has been typed in. The algorithm will then determine which pages it needs to display to the searcher.

All of this takes less than one second to achieve. A person can click on a result by the title, the description below the title, or the web address shown, to determine if that is the site they are looking for. It is worth pointing out that Google does not get paid for organic searches.

Paid Searches

Search engines also show adverts on their pages; most are shown to the side of the organic searches, and a couple will also be shown at the top of the organic search results. These are paid adverts; the search engine has been paid to show the advert, but it's worth noting that they will only show those which are relevant to your search query.

The positioning of each of these adverts is based on bids, that is how much the advertiser is prepared to pay for one single click on their advert; the more they are prepared to pay, the higher up the page the ad will appear. Of course, you can also go down this route, in order to up your presence at the top of the search engine results, but it costs money, and it may be that you can gain your results with slightly less expensive methods.

Every time an ad is clicked, the advertiser pays the agreed price to the search engine. How popular an advert is also has some bearing on where the ad is ranked. The more clicks on a specific advert, the more likely it is to be placed in a prominent position on the page.

Paid searches have absolutely no effect on organic search results for the same company, and vice versa, organic search results do not affect paid search results.

What is organic SEO in simplistic terms?

The aim of this book is to give you an overview of SEO and to give you a detailed understanding at the same time, however we will keep reiterating common terms and areas in more simplistic language, not because I don't believe you will understand, but because understanding completely is the aim; if something is written in technical jargon, you might close this book because you simply don't get it!

My aim is to help you understand completely, so this particular section will give you that quick and easy run down of organic SEO.

The word 'organic' basically tells you what it is we're talking about here – nothing added, no gimmicks, nothing particularly negative, simply website traffic directed to your site by non-paid means. We will discuss paid SEO a lot in this book, and again, we will break it down into a simplistic manner shortly, but organic SEO is free, and it is drummed up by using clever content marketing means, smart use of keywords, and white hat SEO strategies. Organic SEO is also sometimes called 'natural SEO', which basically sums it up in the same way.

What is paid SEO in simplistic terms?

Moving on from organic SEO, we need to break paid SEO down in order to complete the circle.

I really shouldn't have to talk too much about this, because it literally is what it says on the tin; paid SEO comes at a cost, and how much of this you decide to use in your SEO plan is up to you, and totally depends on your budget available. On top of this, paid SEO is about adverts which you see from other businesses also, and they are ways in which search engines also receive revenue – every time you click on one of these adverts, the business to whom the advert belongs, pays the search engine for the privilege.

Google Adwords and any pay per click scheme falls under the umbrella of paid SEO – basically any form of website and traffic marketing which requires you to pay money to bring it in your direction. How much of this you use, as we have mentioned before, depends on your budget.

Chapter 3

The Different SEO Hats

SEO experts do not actually physically wear hats; the word is used as a term to describe the type of SEO they use, and the tactics used.

At one time, SEO tactics were defined entirely by a few search engines, however these days, SEO tactics are controlled and defined entirely by just one search engine, the big daddy of them all - we are talking, of course, about Google.

So, let's look at what an SEO hat is, and what it means.

Hat colors are nothing more than tactics that are used to help a website gain ranking. The color of the hat is determined by the purity of the tactics and how close the terms and conditions of the search engine are stuck to. That really is all it is, unless that SEO expert does not inform their client of the risks. If you choose to hire an SEO professional, they should give you a detailed rundown of the strategy they are going to use, and that way you can assess and be sure that their tactics are as pure as snow, rather than blacker than coal.

If you were performing a risky tactic that could possibly get your client thrown out of the rankings, and you did not tell them about it, you are termed as an unethical SEO, not a black hat SEO – do not confuse the two terms. It is important to always check testimonials before you choose any SEO professional to work with, because this will tell you whether you are looking at an unethical type, or someone who is actually going to help you achieve your optimal SEO needs.

Hats are tactics - the color is the purity of the tactic; the color signifies how closely you have followed the guidelines of the search engine.

Let's take a closer look at the different colors we hear talked about.

White Hat SEO

White hats are 100% pure. This group stay entirely within the terms and service conditions that are set by the search engine (Google in most cases). A white hat SEO does nothing that could risk their client being thrown out of the rankings, and they stick to the speed limit all the way, not even creeping one mile over it. Whilst some may say that sticking to white hat tactics 100% of the time means a harder process, it's always worth noting that white hat tactics will never cause you long-term trouble or strife.

Many SEO professionals choose to go white hat because it is just common sense, however others do it for moral reasons. Going for white hat SEO means that you are not breaking any rules, and this means that whenever an update is issued, your site will likely not be affected at all; this is because the search engine is not looking for you, it's looking for the ones that have broken the rules; basically, white hat means you can sleep easily at night, without worrying about the possibility of being caught out.

A white hat SEO will drive at the speed limit in the right hand lane, while the black hat, driving the black Lamborghini, is being pulled in the left lane for driving 50 miles per hour over the speed limit. Whether that black hat gets a ticket or not depends on whether he or she is actually caught out.

True white hat SEO is as rare as snow in the desert; the reason for this is that almost no SEO professional is prepared to sit and wait for a link profile to build up naturally. In fact, if you were to see a white hat SEO profile that had waited for this to happen naturally, it would likely be extremely fake.

Whether you are building links or buying them, these links are the top way in which the search engine determines how popular your website is. Links will come and links will go, but it is rare that all of the links on your site will be 100% natural.

Grey Hat SEO

Grey hat SEO is all about mixing it up a bit. This is a combination of impatience, budget, and a real lack of understanding; it is a mix of a pure white tactics, following all the rules the search engine chose, with a little dash of something that bends the rules just a little. You could argue that professionals who constantly use grey hat tactics are those who don't truly understand SEO at all, because they are straddling at line that has problems on either side of it.

For example, if you were a pure grey hat SEO, you might use link distribution tactics to build up the links to your site, but you would never consider going down the route of buying those links from a link seller. You might write some fantastic quality content in vast quantities, knowing full well it isn't all relevant, but has substance, some relevance and high quality. What you would never do is use a content spinner.

Grey hat SEO is used to help hasten the results but with the minimum chance of risking penalties from search engines. However, if you are not careful about how you do this, you could find yourself slipping into black hat territory.

Black Hat SEO

Is all black hat SEO evil?

There are actually two forms of black hat SEO, and this is where it all gets somewhat confusing, because definition does not clearly separate them from one another. In addition, depending on what you are working on, both formats can have very different meanings.

For the purpose of this section, I am going to draw a very hard line - Black hat SEO is not actually negative SEO, it is the actual tactics used which are specifically forbidden by your chosen search engine. If, for example, you were using Google, buying links from a link seller would be classed as black hat. If you were using Bing, on the other hand, they would consider purchasing "likes" on your Facebook page, or followers to your Twitter page as black hat.

When a search engine issues a major update, they are generally looking to target the black hatters, and these tactics can seriously harm your website if the search engine roots them out.

Black hat SEO is actually one of the most difficult to achieve because it means having to fly beneath the radar, to never be discovered, and not get your client, or your own website banned from the search engine!

If you cannot do this, 99.999% of the time successfully, never do it on your main website. If you are practicing on burner sites, your success rate has to be at least equal to your pay rate, and the client must know exactly what they have asked you to do for them, and what the risks and penalties are if they, and you, get caught. Using a black hat SEO professional is a risky business, so always think very carefully if you see that the individual you are using is not 100% above board.

Black hat SEO and the quality of the search engine result

So, does any of what I have told you have any bearing on the quality of the results from the search engines? Not yet, no.

Many of the largest companies in the world have used black hat SEO tactics, including BMW, Overstock and JC Penney. Once again, the hats are nothing more than the tactics used to get your website ranked, it's a lot more about whether you get caught out or not, and if you do, the penalties and consequences can be very severe indeed.

In fairness, the lower quality websites do not meet so many of the points that are ticked off on the search engine algorithms. Because of this, they do not use so many of the gray or white hat techniques and tend to lean in the direction of black hat, whereas a site that has fantastic content, great code, a really good design, a high user base, etc., can rank high without risking any kind of penalty – because of this they tend to stay on the lighter side, namely the white and grey varieties.

So, does this mean that sites which are of a lower quality are, in fact, lower sites? No, it does not. I guess the bottom line is that if you can create a top quality website, which we will go over in more detail shortly, then you are on the fast track to improvement already, with no black hat SEO required.

There are an awful lot of "Fortune 500" websites which are really, really bad - simply because their marketing department decided that an unusable website with a nice picture was far better than a site that was user friendly. When an SEO professional talks about quality, they are not talking particularly about the company behind the website, they are talking about how a search engine defines quality.

Now, websites can easily be removed from the search engine index if they are discovered to be using black hat techniques. So does that make those tactics a no go area? Is that what makes back hat SEO evil? No; as I said, black hat is nothing more than a tactic, and the risk comes in whether you get caught or not.

Google, or whichever search engine you have chosen, might not particularly like a tactic you have chosen to use but that does not make it a bad one. The only caveat to this is if the SEO professional does not tell their client what they are doing, and what the risks are. Of course, an additional reason for this is if you are really bad at black hat SEO, and that means you are 99% likely to get caught out.

Now that might sound insulting but, at the end of the day, if you are really bad at black hat SEO and you still continue to use it, you can cause a lot of damage, even more so if your client still does not know about it!

It is worth pointing out that there are plenty of legitimate, true professional SEO experts out there who do use black hat SEO, simply because it is just a tactic and, when used right, it can reap many rewards for the client, the choice of whether you use it or not is up to you.

What about negative SEO?

Also known as competitive leveling, there is one saying that stands out – SPAM stands for "Sites Positioned Above Mine".

These techniques are used to do nothing more than take out the competition, and so that as your website works its way through the ranks, there is less competition for it to wade through on its way to the top. Obviously if there less people in your way, there is more chance of you being top dog.

Think of this as something like blowing up the pathway outside the bricks and mortar buildings of your competition. To some people, this is all just a big part of the search engine game, but be aware that whilst your standing in the ranks may be all that matters to you, some of the tactics used are illegal, and could land you in some very hot water if discovered. I am aware that we keep repeating that fact, but it is the truth, and something you need to be 100% aware of.

It really is much better to do a good job in the first place, better than your opponent, and that way you get the satisfaction of knowing that you are number one in the rankings without cheating, and you also get that comfortable night's sleep as a result.

So, now that you know what hats are, what the colors mean in SEO terms, and what negative leveling is, what do search engines like Google really think of SEO professionals?

Does Google hate the SEO professionals?

Absolutely not!

Think for a minute - Google is home to thousands of trained professionals, people who build their websites exactly the way that Google wants them to. Why would the biggest search engine in the world hate SEO? Placing such a high importance on the search engine is a major big-up for Google, so of course they don't hate those who work to better themselves in their rankings.

Remember this – Google has a product, and that product is the information which it serves up to every person that searches for a keyword or key phrase. If the information they serve up is rubbish, then Google has absolutely no value whatsoever. Google doesn't want that any more than you want your business to go down the pan before it has even got started. Put simply, Google needs good websites and those come from SEO professionals - SEO professionals who follow the terms and conditions laid out by Google; because of this, Google loves SEO professionals!

We are well aware that search engines are far from perfect and, more often than not, a lot of junk finds its way into search results. There are plenty of people who have little to no talent, are uneducated and unknowing, yet they still call themselves SEO experts; it is down to you to make sure that the SEO tactic you use truly works, really does get you the results you are looking for and does it without breaking any rules.

Let's explore exactly what you need to look for when you are hiring a SEO professional.

Putting your website and SEO in the hands of a professional

The huge importance of online marketing is proven by the number of professionals, or otherwise, who will sell you their services in order to tick the boxes you need to drive sales and traffic. You only have to Google the words 'SEO professional' and you will see pages upon pages of people who will try and sell you their services, all promising to give you the best optimization for your particular business needs.

Of course, not everyone is legit, and not everyone is all that experienced in exactly what SEO is, but amongst those dodgy few, you will find some seriously top-notch individuals who will be able to bring you plentiful much-needed traffic to your site, which obviously then equates to cash in your pocket when you make a sale on your goods and services.

Like anything in life, you need to be careful who you work with; a little like hiring someone for a bricks and mortar job role, you need to interview them carefully, even if that isn't in a traditional face to face way.

Follow these tips to find the best man or woman for your job:

Think carefully before you do anything – what do you actually need, and could you do it yourself? Be brutally honest here, could you actually manage your SEO plan yourself, or do you need help? If you feel you can handle it yourself, make sure you actually understand every single facet of what SEO is, and why it is important. You also need to know about strategy plans, and the ins and outs of how to make traffic flow in your direction, and not in the direction of a competitor. If you feel confident, this is somewhere you can save money, because you are obviously going to have to pay professional to do the job for you otherwise, and much of the time these skills don't come cheap!

Write down your needs, i.e. do you have no knowledge whatsoever and you need to start from scratch? Do you know a little and you can bring some input into the strategy you and your professional decide between you? Or are you happy to leave your SEO requirements completely in the hand of your chosen individual? Think about it, write it down, brainstorm it, and come up with a solid plan of what it is you actually need. This will mean you are in a much stronger position when it comes to discussing your ideas with your chosen person, without the risk of getting, shall we say, a little ripped off.

Create a shortlist. Obviously you have checked Google and found a few possible professionals or companies you want to use for your SEO requirements. Never go beyond the first page where this is concerned – think about this in terms of what you're trying to do for your own SEO requirements; you don't want customers or clients to have to trawl through pages upon pages of search results to find your name, because it's unlikely they ever will, and the same can be said for the SEO professional you want to use – if they are good at SEO, then they will be at the top of the search results pages!

Once you have your shortlist of three or four particular companies or individuals you want to use, it's time to start asking questions.

Ask questions! What do you want to know? Do you want to know how they work? Do you want to know how long they envisage the project will take? Do you want to work with them on an ongoing basis? Think about the questions you want answering, and compile an email encompassing them all. Don't forget to ask about the particular strategies they use.

Check out feedback and testimonials. Any good quality SEO professional worth their salt will have testimonials on their website, so make sure you read them. If you find negative ones, steer clear! SEO is not a part of your business which you need to go at with half measures; if you find plentiful positive feedback, then you know you are onto a potential winner.

Ask for samples. Ask them for examples of work they have done in the past, e.g. a website they have worked with, one which has shown success. Have a look at it and see what content and tactics are used.

Aside from asking questions, also don't be afraid to ask tough questions. Obviously don't come out with "do you use black hat tactics" as your opening gambit but it is important to explore this rather murky subject. You need professional in SEO who is above board and who is going to bring you the results you need, in the correct way, without resorting to tactics which could land you in hot water if you are found out. We talked about these tactics in detail in our last section, and whether you go down that road is your decision, but you need to know what you are dealing with from the get-go.

Once you settle on a candidate, brief them in full about your website and service requirements. It's important for your SEO professional to understand your business in its entirety, and not just to have a loose grip on what products and services you offer. Of course, they're not going to be the ones who are actually dealing with the day to day business side of things, but they have to know what it is you do in order to drive the correct traffic and sales towards your bank account.

Set a probation period. Work together for, say, three months first, and see if you find results are desirable or not. If you don't notice a difference, it may be time to head back to that shortlist you had previously and pick the next candidate down.

Of course, you could cut all of this process out by working through your SEO needs yourself, but if you are going to do that, make sure you give yourself ample time and space to actually dedicate the effort required, and the time that such a large responsibility really does deserve.

Chapter 4

The Different Types of SEO

Whilst there are several different SEO hat colours, indicating the type of SEO they are, there are also several different types of SEO; this is something that not many beginners to the arena realize.

One thing I do want to point out is, if you don't have all of the skills needed for all of the different type of SEO, you can still use them, however, I would recommend, quite strongly, that you start by building up your skills for one type at a time. Again, we will shortly simplify each type at the end of this section, to reiterate knowledge and understanding, so don't worry if you don't quite grasp it the first time around.

There is a theory amongst the professional, top SEOs that if a person can't configure an Apache Web server, then they are simply not a real SEO expert; this is almost like saying that, if you have never practiced brain surgery, then you are not a real doctor (even if you are). There are lots of different areas of specialization in the field of search engine optimization, just like there is in any area of expertise, and each specialized area has its own set of skills that you need to learn

The following list of SEO areas is by no means exhaustive; these are just what are seen as the most important areas to learn - pick one, learn it, learn it again until you know how it works, and how to apply it successfully, before you move on to the next one.

Analytical SEO

Analytical SEO is all about proper keyword research and the analysis of trends. Pretty much every area of SEO audit will fall under the title of analytical SEO and, although that does mean there is a bit of an overlap between this and technical SEO, that will not cause any problems; none of these specializations are completely isolated from the others, and much of the time they actually work together in harmony.

An SEO analyst will spend much of his or her time identifying good opportunities, assessing the needs of their websites and matching up assets to the particular needs identified. In fact, it is safe to say that many SEO strategists rely quite heavily on the full skill set of the analytical SEO.

As well as researching keywords and auditing websites, the analytical SEO will also be involved in analyzing search engine algorithms, and evaluating the available analytic tools and competitive SEO. It is also quite safe to say that professional who uses analytical SEO heavily, is a hard-working type!

SEO Production

The area of SEO production relies heavily on skills in coding and design. Instead of searching out problems to solve, you are working closely with developers or creating your website structures that are fully optimized for SEO. You will be concentrating on the structure, the content, the tools needed, and the widgets.

For the most part, search engine optimization production is concerned with ensuring that, no matter what is produced by a website or on behalf of that website, it does actually play a valuable part in the optimization process.

One area of SEO production would be coming up with and creating new "SEO plugins" for both Drupal and WordPress installations, however SEO production is more focused on creating the basis for growth in the future. If this all sounds a little technical at first, don't worry, because this is certainly an area that any good SEO professional will know about.

The area of SEO production is likely to produce the best results for those websites that fell foul of the downgrades to Google's Panda algorithms.

Technical SEO

Technical SEO is all about searching for problems, specifically those that are "under the hood". One of the most important skills in this area is to be able to evaluate applications and codes which work together to provide both search engines and users with content.

Technical SEO is NOT about planning and it is not about coming up with websites that are fully optimized – it is all about fixing issues that stop the websites from achieving a top performance level.

Theoretical Search Engine Optimization

Most SEO experimentation and testing falls under this title but you must also include a number of other areas, such as keeping up to date on current research and the latest in search engine patents. Just about anything that is associated with the retrieval of information is covered under this and it all comes together to provide a framework that you can use to understand exactly what the Searchable Web Ecosystem is, and how it works.

Theoretical SEO will follow the web crawlers, looking for the good ones and separating them out from the bad ones, as well as looking to understand exactly what the best practices are for managing crawl. Like any theoretical discovery area, theoretical SEO has opened up some pretty spectacular failures, including widespread failures in practices for search engine optimization.

The following list of failures is just a glimpse:

- **PageRank Hoarding** – the practice of trying to stop PageRank from leaving a website, something which is pretty much impossible
- **PageRank Sculpting** – the practice of attempting to drive the flow of PageRank through a particular website
- **Link-Driven Search Performance** – otherwise known as "ranking through links"
- **Content Marketing** - this led to the Panda update which knocked an awful lot of websites for six. More on content marketing will follow later.

Strategic Search Engine Optimization

Strategic search engine optimization takes everything you learn from all the other areas and tries to apply it all in a highly practical way. It does this by coming up with brand new strategies that are focused on future marketing and optimization.

An example of a strategy could be to come up with a number of new websites that cover a particular topic, and then to promote the websites using social media to try and draw attention and interest. Another strategy might be to publish a website that has very little content on it and then to start pointing links towards the websites, as many as possible.

Strategic search engine optimization also tries to anticipate any changes to the way the Searchable Web Ecosystem works, although it doesn't actually have to do this. In short, strategic SEO simply churns out strategies based on formulae for individual websites, and these are often termed as "marketing blueprints", action plans", marketing plans", etc.

Link Building is not SEO

In a technical or a moral sense, there is nothing wrong with link building. At the end of the day, the world wide web would not exist in its current format without links, and we are all free to go looking for and asking for links back to our websites. The earliest known online marketing practices actually relied very heavily on link building because, at the time, web advertising and web searches were simply not adequate enough.

However, if you base your entire search engine marketing strategy on links, I can tell you now that you are doomed for failure. Put simply, this is an extremely simple-minded strategy which has now been underlined by the changes that both Bing and Google have made to their algorithms, changes that confirm what most of us have known for many years – search engines will always react quickly to manipulative and abusive practices that are widespread, such as link building. In short, link building is very easy to spot, so you are basically stood waving your arms around, shouting "catch me!" if you do this.

Now, that isn't to say that all link builders are manipulative; some of them use the practice sensibly and within the guidelines set out by the search engines, but there are those who fill their websites and others with links, many of which are not good ones, simply to try and raise their ranking. Search engineers are much, much better now than ever before at tracking down these manipulative links, and this will result in negative rankings and feedback for you.

If you want to base your strategy on links that are not manipulative, that is fine, but, in all honesty, most of the websites out there today will not see any return on it. It is a fine balancing act; your resources have to be balanced between website design, content production, the acquisition of links and interacting with your users – therefore the least efficient way to market your website is through link acquisition; keep this to a minimum as much as possible, and use it sparingly.

Off-site SEO is real

Off-site SEO is very real, but a lot of people equate it purely to link building. Off-site SEO is about far more than just acquiring links, and those people who spend all or most of their time on building or earning links have very poor off-site SEO, and in truth, very poor SEO in general as a result.

Off-site SEO is also about building up website visibility, encouraging discussions about the site, and building query space. Off-site SEO actually relies more heavy on real content marketing, on creating real visibility and traffic which falls outside the normal marketplace. You simply cannot target specific keywords for your particular niche and still use content marketing; targeting keywords that are out of niche is not efficient, and it is not as effective for many websites as it is to use off-site SEO.

Another form of off-site SEO is guest posting, even if that guest post doesn't give you a link back to your own website. You can write great guest posts in a niche or industry that is not even remotely related to yours, making no mention whatsoever of your website and still stimulate a lot of interest amongst people who are looking for areas that are your specialty. Networking is key in this business.

Chapter 5

The Difference Between Social Media and Content Marketing

Believe it or not, there are still a lot of people who are not familiar with content marketing, and indeed, many confuse it with social media marketing as soon as they learn that content marketing is about brands and content publishing. The two areas are separate to each other, and it is important to understand in detail what content marketing is, as well as how you can use social media to your advantage too.

There is no doubt that content marketing does rely extensively on social media these days, and we know that businesses use social media to publish content which gets their message across. Whilst there is some overlap between the two, they are both very different marketing strategies - each has its own focal points, its own processes and its own goals. The important thing to remember is that social media accounts should always be linked to and from your actual website, in order to pull everything together and create that circle of attention you need, to push your site to the top of the search engine rankings.

To help you understand the differences, important when you are drawing up your SEO strategy, let's take a look at the ways in which they are different from one another, whilst also simplifying content marketing at the same time.

Market Activity Focus

Also known as the "center of gravity", in social media marketing this is kept within the social media network. When a marketer runs a social media marketing campaign, they are working inside Twitter, Facebook, LinkedIn, Pinterest, or any social media site that they choose, and whenever they come up with new content, they will publish it on one or more of those sites. If you update your Facebook page with a particular promotion, you need to Tweet it, you need to add it on every other social media site you have, and you need to ensure it is linked onto your website – it is a circle that never needs to break.

By direct contrast, content marketing is centered firmly on a particular brand website, be it a fully branded URL, such as AmericanExpress.com, or a microsite related to a specific product for a brand, such as Amex's Open Forum. Whilst social media networks are important to the ultimate success of a content marketing campaign, social networks are not used as containers for the content; instead they are merely the vehicle by which the links to the content are distributed, sending visitors straight to the brand website. We know that social media is huge these days, so you should certainly be taking advantage of it, whilst also understanding the subtle differences between this and content marketing in its purest form.

Content Types

With a social media network, marketing content is built explicitly for the platform being used – Twitter allows short messages of 140 characters, Facebook allow the use of games, quizzes and contests, etc. On a social media site, the brand is modeling how they behave around that of the people who use the networks.

Content marketing is somewhat different in that the content can be much longer, based on the content of the website. A brand can publish just about any type of content, such as a blog post, a full length article, videos, eBooks, infographics, and many more formats besides. In content marketing, the brand is modelling their behavior around that of the media publishers.

Objectives

Both content marketing and social media marketing can be used for any number of purposes, whereas social media marketing tends to aim its focus on two objectives – brand awareness, and customer satisfaction/retention. Brand awareness on social media is all about generating discussions and activity around your particular brand, and you can also use these networks as a kind of open forum where you can talk directly with your customers; you can answer any questions they may have to solve any issues that may arise, allowing you the chance to retain your customers and keep them happy. Social media is a good way of speaking to your customers on a personal basis, without it being a formal question and answer session, or a long page of text which they may not feel engaged to read to the end of.

By direct contrast, content marketing is focused mainly on the generation of demand. The higher the quality of the content you publish on your website; the more prospects are brought to the site, and this allows you to develop a relationship with those prospects, and help them on their way to a purchase, or a lead conversion. As you can see, the two are subtly different, but they work together closely, in order to push traffic and interest to your website.

The evolution of online marketing

It is very difficult to work out the ratio of brands that use social media marketing compared to the brands that prefer content marketing, however, it is most likely in the favor of social media marketing, since that is the topmost thought of virtually all marketing departments. Content marketing used to be the favored way and is now making a very strong comeback however, and used in conjunction with social media networks, it could very well see a huge leap in use. Put simply, social media is bang on trend right now, so of course businesses are going to go down that route, however content marketing should certainly not be forgotten in its own right.

At the end of the day, now that social media is a major part of everyday life, the two marketing strategies are no longer isolated entities; instead they are two parts of the evolution of online marketing. The Internet has opened the way for every single brand to be able to communicate with their customers directly, without needing to use industry intermediaries, and to keep things more personal and direct.

The first and most natural step in the process is social media marketing. People spend vast amounts of time on social sites and that makes access to customers easy. Content can be cut down into smaller chunks, making it easy to publish. Think about how much time people spend on sites like Facebook every single day, and then think about how many millions of people use it – that's a huge amount of people you can reach with just one quick strategy, and regular updates.

However, as brands start to familiarize themselves with their role of publisher, there will be a natural move towards content marketing. The bar is set much higher here because brands have to be able to produce content that is much higher in quality, and the longer they need to be able to build up their audience on their website. In short, they will become the true meaning of a media publisher, despite the fact it takes longer to build up.

However, although the bar is set higher, the rewards are far greater in content marketing and far more powerful.

Content marketing allows a brand to engage very deeply with their customers, and by driving the traffic to the website, they have a much larger opportunity to pick up leads and convert them.

What is content marketing in simplistic terms?

"A strategic approach to marketing which is focused on creating and then distributing relevant and valuable content, which is consistent, with the aim to attract and then retain an audience which is clearly defined. This ultimately drives profitable action from customers".

Easy, right?

Don't over-complicate things, the clue is in the title.

Content marketing is about marketing your website, which basically markets your goods and services, using content you publish on your site. This could take the form of videos, pictures, gifs, blog posts, articles, basically any content which is targeted to your particular audience.

Of course, you need to know who your audience are in the first place, but this is probably something you did when you put together your very first business plan. Knowing who your customers are, who your overall audience are, and what they want to see and need, is the number one key to being able to push your marketing efforts in the correct direction; it's no good pushing your goods and services at the wrong people, you're basically wasting time and money if you do that.

Figure out who your audience are, find out what they want, what they like, and what content they respond best to, e.g. if you have a young audience, you might find they enjoy You Tube videos, and if you have an older audience, you might find they like more written content. Once you know what your audience like, you are in a much better position to give it to them.

Keeping the customer happy here is key.

How do you identify the best content for your website?

Again, you need to know what your customers want, and then target your approach to them. If you go down the road of blog posts, you need a consistent voice, i.e. you need the same person to do the blogging every single time. You can't have a blog post with one particular writing voice, perhaps writing in the first person, in a chatty way, and then switch to a scientific and formal voice for the next post – this is only going to confuse your audience, and confusion causes a major turn off.

Stick to consistency, and figure out how your customers like to be spoken to, i.e. is it a chatty approach? Do they prefer a formal conversation? Is it something in the middle that reaches out and touches your audience better? Think about this carefully, do your research, and tailor your approach accordingly.

Content marketing is not difficult, and once you identify what content is going to work for you and your audience, you simply need to be consistent, keep your content uploaded regularly (although not too much, because too much content can be distracting), and make sure that anything you do post is relevant to your business and the situation at the time.

Social media – the biggest player on the Internet scene

Can you remember a time before Facebook? Do you remember how you used to spend your spare time? Many of us can't, I certainly wonder sometimes how I would get through a day without checking my messages or how many 'likes' my latest selfie attracted, and I'm sure many of you are the same.

Despite that rather fun side of social media, there is also a very profitable side too.

Put simply, social media gives you a voice to millions of people, and out of those millions of people you could find that many of them are potential customers.

Potential customers mean potential money in your pocket, through the medium of online sales, and word of mouth marketing.

If you don't make use of social media then you are seriously missing out, and you are allowing your business to suffer as a result.

Get yourself onto the major social media sites and watch your traffic improve massively.

Now, which sites should you be paying the most attention to?

It's important to ask this question because every week there seems to be a new social media site on the block, and whilst most of them don't last very long, or don't seem to be very successful at all, there are a few which have grown into major industry players – Facebook being the most important and most commonly used.

Facebook

Okay, so it's not about selfies and 'likes', it's about reaching potential customers, we agree on this. Now, the first thing you need to do in order to reach those potential customers is to create a business page and then market the hell out of it. Whether you choose to do this yourself or you hire a virtual assistant or social media expert to do this for you, this is basically a personal choice, and comes down to how skilled you are in this area, and how much of a budget you have available.

Sharing is the most powerful tool on Facebook, and you can also easily update your site with new promotions and news. Ask people to share it onwards from there, and perhaps even go for a sponsored ad status, at a price of course.

Once you have established your business page, you need to link it onto your website, and as with any content on your site, you need to update your Facebook page regularly – nobody likes a page with no updates, however nobody likes a page with too many updates either!

Twitter

Whilst Twitter certainly isn't as easy to understand as Facebook, once you get to grips with the basics, you will quickly see it's potential.

Twitter basically allows you to send quick messages, or 'tweets' to your followers, which can then be 're-tweeted' and sent on, hopefully with the aim of going viral.

The same rules we have just discussed about Facebook basically apply here – set yourself up with an account, make it eye-catching, and then tweet regularly, whilst also getting involved in other conversations, and with a back-link to your particular account. Obviously, make sure any conversations you do get involved in are relevant to your business, and avoid anything controversial, but with the millions of people who see these conversations will then click on your particular address, and see your profit – hey presto! Potential customers to your website, which will obviously be linked back to your particular website also.

YouTube

Create yourself a YouTube channel and update regularly with videos and demonstrations on your products. You could also throw in the odd fun item too, just to up the attention-grabbing side of your account.

Never underestimate the power of YouTube – when people are bored, they search YouTube for entertainment, so this is your chance to be their entertainment, whilst also subtly throwing in the marketing for your goods and services, in the direct of your website.

These are just three of the main social media websites you need to have a strong presence on, and of course, remember to link to them all on your website. There are countless other sites, including LinkedIn or Pinterest, which are much more business-orientated, and certainly two sites you need to be present on also.

Whether you love social media or not, the fact remains that in order to reach the maximum number of potential customers possible, you need to get used to the fact that social media is certainly here to stay for a very long time indeed.

Chapter 6

SEO Obstacles You Will Fall Over

As with anything in life, there are always obstacles to your success. One of the biggest obstacles to SEO, and one of the single biggest challenges, is getting the balance right.

Your content has to satisfy the visitors to your site and the search engines. Whilst your web page content may be highly entertaining to the people that read it, the search engine may not even pick up on it, and that is why each and every page on your website, every piece of content that you write and publish, must be optimized for search engines.

However, sometimes a site that has been fully optimized for search engines can come across as somewhat dry and not very interesting to readers. The best way is to create content is to ensure it is engaging first, and then tweak it so it can be picked up by the search engines. We are going to talk in a lot of detail across this chapter about how to write engaging content, as well as the issue of hiring a freelancer to write for you. You could of course do this yourself, and save cash, so we will also talk about how to seamlessly insert key words, and develop your writing skills to a higher standard.

One of the biggest problems lies with the way that the spiders crawling the sites deal with media files, like videos and photographs. Most people want to see interesting videos and eye-catching photographs on the websites they are looking at; they do not want to be faced with nothing but text, because they will soon get bored and go off looking for something better. Unfortunately, many of the search engines ignore images and videos when they index a website, and this is a huge problem for the website that uses media to get their message across. Some of the more interactive websites have little in the way of text and that doesn't give the spiders very much to feed on when they are indexing the sites.

It is, therefore, understandably tempting for websites that rely on media to turn to black hat techniques to give them something of a chance, however, that normally turn out to be a bad decision on their behalf, if they are caught out.

For a start, the biggest search engines are always updating and upgrading their spider software to better detect and ignore those sites that use black hat tactics; worst case, they will even penalize the site for doing so. The best approach here is to use strategically placed keywords; placed in the page title, the first and last paragraphs of any content and in their Meta descriptions. They should also work on getting links from other websites that are focused on content which is relevant.

It isn't always very easy to optimize a website, and it certainly isn't always straightforward. This is why some people choose to use an SEO consultant, a professional who has been doing this for years. If you choose to go down this route, there are some things you must do – always check the credentials of the SEO consultant before you hire them, look at their track record and the list of clients they have, and make sure you are fully up to date and informed about any SEO issues. If, for example, your SEO consultant recommends a black hat approach and you agree with it, the search engines can hold both of you entirely responsible and accountable – that spells big trouble. Again, we will talk in more detail shortly about what to look for when hiring a professional to work for you.

Many of the SEO companies out there are totally legitimate. They will only use white hat tactics and will help you to turn your web page layout into something that the search engines will see; they will help you to choose the correct keywords, and help you with their placement to gain the best result. They will also help you to facilitate exchanges of links between sites that have complementary content. If you are at all unsure about what you are doing, look for one of these SEO consultants; someone who can truly help you increase your ranking on the search engine results pages.

Using a freelancer to write content, and why they need to be experienced in SEO

As with many areas of life, sometimes you are just not skilled in a particular area, and no matter how much you try to obtain these skills and find a way through, your particular efforts will not match those of someone who has had the skill from birth.

It's true what people say – sometimes you are born with a particular skill, something which is your niche, so to say. In terms of writing content for websites, this is one of those areas where you might not find yourself creating some of the best written content out there, and it could well be that you need to find someone with the skills in a more natural way, to help you out.

We have talked in length previously about how it is very important to ensure any content which goes onto your site is high quality, relevant, perfect in terms of spelling and grammar, and which is updated regularly, with eye-catching and attention grabbing headings. Of course, you also need to throw in the SEO keywords and placement into content; not only do you have to figure out how to actually write great content, but you have to remember SEO as well!

It can be a difficult road to walk on, and that is why it is sometimes better to find someone else to do it for you.

You won't struggle to find a freelance writer, but what you do need is a freelance writer who knows about SEO, and someone who is skilled and adept at inserting keywords into the correct place, without it seeming spammy or false. Nobody wants to read an article or blog post which is blatantly there for marketing,

So, how do you find the ideal person for the job?

You head online, that's what.

Make sure you find a top quality freelancer website, such as Upwork, which is one of the most commonly used. Once you've created an account and created a job, you will find many individuals apply, but in order to find your perfect fit, you need to look at the following areas and criteria:

Look at their rating and feedback. Anyone can claim to be able to write, and anyone can tell you that they are hard-working and would be an asset to your business, but how many of them are actually what they say they are? Check former client feedback, and whilst it is important to take some of it with a pinch of salt (everyone is allowed one fall-down or bad client), if there is constantly bad ratings or feedback given, then steer clear.

Are they new? Whilst it's a great opportunity to give a new writer a foot-up the ladder, it might be wise to go for a more experienced writer if you want to kick-start your website marketing campaign in a quicker manner.

Set your budget. You are able to give a budget for the job, and you can pick your freelancer from those who bid for lower prices. Of course, don't go too far down the budget range, as you may find that the best writers simply won't apply, so be wise with how much you are willing to pay. Remember that you do get what you pay for in many respects, so have a little respect also for the person whose skills you are going to be taking extreme advantage of.

Ask about their knowledge and understanding of SEO. This is so important! If you choose a new writer, they may not be that experienced in SEO, and indeed they may not even know what it is. You really do need to find a writer who understands the importance of working with search engines, and someone who is able to seamlessly and naturally insert keywords into content, in order to drive traffic towards your website. On top of this, a thorough knowledge of the overview of SEO will help also, because that way they are able to write content which is targeted to driving traffic and sales, rather than a 'hit and hope' approach.

Do you want to find a long-term working relationship? It's always wise to stick with the same writer for the duration of your website's lifespan, because that way the writing voice will be consistent, and your readers will not notice any change in tone. Not everyone writes in the same way, so even if you switch your writer up a few times, your readers will tell the difference.

Consistency is key in holding someone's attention for a long period of time. Of course, if you work with the same writer of a long period of time, you are building up trust, and that means you know that you're not going to be let down by someone new, who you don't really know very well at all.

Set out a probationary period. As with finding an SEO professional to work with, you also need to set out a probation period for your writer. Make sure you don't set this too short, but don't make it too long either, otherwise irreversible damage could be done if the writer is shown to be sub-standard. If you are blogging, then perhaps two weeks is a good period of time, because that would equate to around four blog posts, and by that time you can get a solid feel of how things are likely to pan out in the future.

Ask for a test article/blog post. Again, this is simply setting your stall out and seeing what it is you're likely to be getting in the future. When you find someone you would like to hire, after discussing the job in detail first of course, ask for a test piece to be done, so you can see if they really are up to the job.

Communicate regularly and ask for input. You might not be seeing things quite as your writer does, so it's important to have regular catch ups, in order to touch base. Set aside a Skype get-together once a month or so, and brainstorm ideas for new content. You can easily thrash out any issues in this way also, which cuts down on potential problems with your working relationship and the way your website is handled.

Finding the best possible writer for your website isn't a hit and hope kind of approach, and it is something you need to give some serious thought and attention to. Think about it – the person you choose is going to be speaking to your customers first hand, so you need to know that they are going to speak in the correct tone and voice, in order to relate to your client base.

If your target audience are elderly, they are not going to appreciate someone who speaks with a very youthful voice, someone who uses a humorous and modern approach; on the other hand, if your audience is young and hip, they aren't going to appreciate a formal voice either. It's all about knowing who your customers are, and knowing what they want, in order to give it to them.

How to add keywords into your content seamlessly

We have talked about how important it is to get any content right which goes onto your website, and we have also talked about the possibility of hiring a freelance writer to do this for you, especially a writer who has an understanding of SEO and how to use it. Now, if you decide to write the content yourself, then you also need to know how to make use of keywords in a seamless and natural way, whilst also ensuring that the content you create is relevant, quality, and unique.

Again, we have mentioned this, you don't want to write content which seems like it is literally marketing material, because people will simply throw their hands up in the air and say "boring!" Instead, you need to create content which is inspiring, attention-grabbing, and eye-catching, whilst also throwing in those keywords, as though they were simply meant to be there.

It's a difficult thing to get right if you don't know how to do it, but once you have experience, you will find that the process flows much easier.

We discussed about Google AdWords, and how to identify the keywords which best suit your niche, so I won't go over that again, however what I will speak about now is how to insert them into your content without making your writing sound like you are simply throwing in words for the sake of it.

Identify your keywords and topic. Obviously you need to make sure that the topic you have picked to write about will allow insertion of the keyword without it sounding ridiculously out of place. The best advice is to look at the words you need to put in and work out a topic from there, not the other way around.

Write a brief outline for your content. This will allow you to add in your words in the most natural way. Identify what each paragraph is going to talk about, and then figure out from there where to put the keyword, or words, in.

Scatter the keywords equally. You don't want a drenching of the keyword in the first half of the article/blog post, and then nothing until the end. Make sure you insert the keyword naturally and regularly throughout the article, without concentrating it too much in one area.

Where you need to put the keyword(s) – You should mention it once in the title, once in the subtitle, a few times naturally and evenly distributed through the main body of the test, and again in the meta description you create for the search engine.

Use a plug-in to give you an overview of your keyword density. I've talked about which apps and plug-ins you can use to identify how evenly spread your keyword distribution is, so make sure you use this tool, to give you the best information.

Re-read your content after you have written it. Read the article or blog back afterwards and see if it flows, without sounding like the keyword is mentioned too many times, or in an unnatural way. A good tip is to get someone else to read it, someone who doesn't know what the keyword is, to see if they pick up on the frequency of a word being mentioned throughout the content. If they don't notice it, then you've done a good job!

SEO is certainly not all about keywords, and there is more to it than that, but there is also no denying that keywords are vital in pushing your website up in the search engine search results. If you can get onto that first page, your traffic will soar, and that is basically the aim of SEO in general.

Chapter 7

Top 10 SEO Tips for Marketing Your Startup

Getting SEO right is particularly important for the startup business. Marketing today is nothing like it was 10 years ago, and even 2 years ago, to be fair. So much has changed in that it is no longer easy to get past the search engines and become successful without having to consider SEO, and how it will work in relation to your website. If you choose to ignore SEO, you might as well pack up and go home now.

The Internet has a brand new face and with that goes the need for a completely new strategy in terms of developing SEO campaigns that work, in order to keep your website in the eye of the search engine spiders. We talked a lot in previous chapters about giving the spiders the food they need, so they index your site and allow it to show up in search engine search results, and SEO is exactly what does that.

The top 10 SEO tips for getting your startup business noticed are:

1. Work out your target keywords

Good SEO research begins with keywords. To determine your optimal keywords, you must carry out an in-depth analysis of search trends, current and recent past, as well as taking demographics into account. You are looking for target keywords that will give you the most amount of return with the least amount of competition. You need to get your readers interested in what you are writing and publishing and, as any good content marketer will inform you, this is the very first step to building up a relationship with your target audience. Of course, as we have mentioned before, you also need to make sure that readers don't notice the repetitive nature of keywords in your content, to avoid a marketing voice to anything you publish on your site.

2. Make your website mobile friendly

This really is absolutely necessary if you want to get anywhere in today's mobile world. Having a mobile friendly website is the new standard and that has been completely backed up by the latest update from search engine giant, Google. However, the biggest mistake that many website owners make is in thinking that they have to completely rebuild their website to make it usable on mobile devices - this simply isn't true. There are lots of ways to convert your existing website into a mobile friendly one without spending a vast amount of money to do so. Even if money is a concern of yours, not making your site mobile-friendly will cost you far more than it will to make it mobile.

We spend so much time on our phones that of course, whilst people are sat on the bus going to work, or sat waiting for an appointment, they are going to sit and peruse the Internet - make sure you don't miss out on this money-making scheme.

3. **Keep it simple**

When you create content for your startup, you need to be able to make a strong connection with your audience. The best way to do this is to keep things simple - put your message across in a nice, simple way, and in a readable way. At the end of the day, many of the people you are talking to are not going to be industry experts and, if you use too much technical jargon, you will lose them very quickly. In the ideal world, your content will read simply enough for someone who has no background in the industry to understand it perfectly.

The best test of this is to ask someone else to read what you have written, before you go live with it. This person needs to have no knowledge of your service or product, to give you the ideal test of whether your content is relatable.

4. **Develop a proper marketing strategy and follow it**

A good marketing strategy will let you set an end goal to work to, with other goals in between. It will take your target demographic into account, the number of blog posts or social media posts you are going to do each day or week, what your content is going to do, and you can then solve problems when your content does not work as you expected it to. Marketing strategies are never set in stone; they will constantly move, the goalposts will change and you must be ready to move with it. Before it can do that though, you have to make the development of your marketing strategy plan one of your very first jobs. Don't be too rigid, allow yourself to make mistakes, but always ensure that you correct them afterwards.

5. **Use the power of infographics**

In the last few years, infographics have grown to become one of the most popular forms of media used in content, and they are also one of the most popular forms of content shared on social media sites. The reason for their success is very simple – infographics are incredibly powerful, using both graphics and text to grab the attention of the reader and pull them into your content. The combination of the two is far more powerful than either one on their own, so always make sure you take advantage of this.

6. **Get your priorities right**

The single biggest mistake that rookie businesses make when they set up their marketing strategy is not getting their priorities in order. No matter what your business is, the most important facet, the most important resource that you have, is time. In order to be able to manage your time effectively, you have to be aware of what needs to be done first and then balance it with what is going to have the most impact on your target audience. There really isn't anything to be gained from doing something in a highly efficient and effective manner if it didn't need doing in the first place; don't waste time, because time certainly is money.

7. **Work out which social channels you will use**

There are so many social media channels that it can be difficult to work out where to go to get the best impact. Some people fall into the trap of trying to use them all and find that, as per the above point, their most important resource is being used up on things that really are not necessary. A little bit of research will root out the best channels for you to use, the ones where most of your target audience spend their time - that is where your attention needs to be directed. We talked about the most common social media sites to use previously, so choose these main ones, and then filter through the others accordingly.

8. **Build your links**

These days, link building requires that you have a proper understanding of how things like anchor tags work. You also need to have a solid understanding of how to use them to raise your search engine ranking. One of the keys to working out which websites are the best ones to link to is to work out link relevancy. There are plenty of tools, free and paid, that allow you to see very quickly if a link has any benefit or is any good; this is vital because the links that you choose signify your websites' relevancy to your particular niche. Using a tool such as this also saves time wasting and potential costly mistakes.

9. **Your content must be relevant**

If you are producing content about a specific topic within your niche, you must do everything necessary, everything that the topic is covering. Your content is what is going to attract new users to your website, so keeping it high in quality and completely relevant is going to stop your website from stagnating. This also gives weight to the idea of generating high quality backlinks that go with high quality content and, together, all of this makes for a good rank on the search engine page rankings. On top of this, any images you use must speak about the content you are writing about; nobody is going to have trust or confidence in a business who simply throw images at content, which has no relevancy at all.

10. **Analytics really are your friend**

Numbers do not tell lies, and the numbers that are relevant to you will tell you all about your website, which bits are successful and which bits aren't. While it is important to celebrate the successes, you must never ignore the failures. In truth, these numbers are probably more important because these are the ones that help you to see where you are going wrong, and give you valuable information to indicate where you can improve your website. Analytics give you some good goals to work towards, and are an excellent guide to whether your marketing campaign is working as it should be. Don't get too downcast when you see an area that is failing; turn this into a positive and see it as an opportunity for improvement.

The importance of a good quality website

It is all very well and good talking about SEO, and what you should and shouldn't do, but if you don't have a top quality website to promote in the first place, what is the point of any of it? We are going to talk about this several times across this book, and we will reiterate each point a few times also, which should tell you a lot about how important it truly is.

If your website is full of broken links, it's boring to look at, hard to find your way around, and basically doesn't give the customer much information, then you're not going to find visitors heading back to your site once they've looked at it once; you're certainly not going to get any shares or likes on Facebook, and people aren't going to give you that all important word of mouth promotion either.

Can you now see how important it is to give some serious thought to your ground work?

Let's head back to the basics.

Okay, so you want to promote your goods or services through the medium of the Internet.

Good choice. Everyone is online these days, whether they want to be or not, and this literally opens up the world for your business. In order to keep people visiting your site, and to avoid them turning off completely, here are a few tips to follow:

Make sure the format and design reflects your business. Yes, you might want to go all colorful and fancy, but if your product or service isn't really about that, then you're basically not understanding your own niche, whilst also confusing your customers in the process. Choose a design which says something about who you are; if your product is fun and light-hearted, go for a colorful and fun design, if your product is more serious, go for something which is a little more formal. It's all about knowing who you are, so you can easily inform others.

Write down what you want to have on your site. Too many pages and nobody will ever navigate their way around them all, too little and you're not giving enough information. Have a brainstorming session and write down the key pages you need to have on your site; these should include:

- An eye-catching front page - this could show current promotions and sales advertisements.
- About Us – Tell your customers a little about who you are and what you do, including how long you've been doing it.
- Testimonials – Everyone loves to read about an experience a former customer has had with your business, so make sure you ask happy customers to leave you a review; this will drive future business your way.
- FAQ – Everyone also love to have their frequently asked questions answered, so make sure you think about this and compile a list of things which you are asked regularly. Make sure your answers are comprehensive and actually

answer the question, without going around the houses.

- Contact Us – A regularly checked email account address, telephone number(s), postal address, and links to your social media accounts, including Facebook, Twitter etc. You could also have a section here which allows customers to submit questions to your site – you can download a widget for this quite easily.
- A blog. Blogs are powerful tools, and they speak to your customers on a personal level. You could have your blog actually on your website page, or you could link to it; basically whichever works for you, however having your blog actually on this page cuts out the messing around for your customers.
- Your actual product information. This could be your online catalogue, whereby customers buy their products, or it could be in-depth information on what you sell/provide.

Make sure all your links actually work. It's no good have links to different parts of your website, or even external links to other sites, if they don't work when a customer clicks on them. Think about this from your point of view – how many times have you clicked on link and found it broken? Did you go back to the site again? Or did you get frustrated and simply give up and go somewhere else? I'm guessing you went somewhere else, which is what your customers will do if you don't check your links are working regularly.

Update your site regularly. If you have a blog on your site then you need to blog around least twice per week, however don't do it too much because otherwise it gets too repetitive. In terms of your front page, make sure you update this regularly too with new offers and news. If your site is stagnant for too long, people will forget about it, and nobody will go back to it. Forgotten websites do not drive sales forward.

If you have no idea how to build a website, get someone else to do it for you. Yes, you can save money by doing it yourself, and it's quite easy to do too, but if you have no idea where to start, and you're not really sure what you're doing, it's false economy to drive forward in a DIY manner. You can easily hire a freelancer to design and build your website for you, making use of their specialized skills to help you create a strong and powerful site for future use.

Equally, if you don't have the time to maintain the site, you could hire a virtual worker to do your website work for you. The pros of this are that you don't need to actually hire them in a conventional way, i.e. you don't have to provide a desk, computer, pay for electric and heating etc, because you hire them online, as a freelancer, in a virtual way. This frees you up to work on other parts of the business, and again, you can make use of specialized skills, which you might not have.

Cut out the waffle. If you build pages and update for the sake of it, with no real aim to the whole procedure, then your customers are going to see straight through it. Make sure everything you put on your website it concise, and make sure you actually have a voice. By this, I mean that you are speaking to your customers in the same way every time – don't use the first person for one update, and then switch to the third person; be consistent and your customers will see this as a genuine person speaking to them. Any content you put on your website has to be of a high quality, because any errors in spelling and grammar will be picked up on, and this is a huge vote of no confidence for customers. How many times have you read something on a flyer or website and picked up on a mistake? Did it leave you with a feeling of confidence? I'm guessing not.

Put simply, you could have the best SEO plan in the world, but if your website isn't up to scratch, there really is no point in going ahead with it. Combine your SEO efforts with a top quality website and you really are on the road to success.

Chapter 8

Top 10 SEO Secrets to Dominating the First Page

In a nutshell, the answer to dominating the first page of the search engine ranking lies in content marketing - it is a simple as that.

Let me explain that a little further.

Despite the hype and the rumors that flood the web every day, it really isn't all that hard to improve on your search engine rankings, really, it isn't. We've all read the lies that tell us how difficult search engine optimization really is, and so many people live with these lies, believing in them. It is because of this school of thought that SEO seems so difficult but, if you let go of the hype and go your own way, you will find it isn't so difficult after all, especially of you follow the 10 secrets I divulge here.

By reading this book so far, you should certainly see that the whole business of SEO can be simplified, provided you focus on what you need to do, as well as understanding why you need to do it. The aim is that by this point, you will be feeling a lot more hopeful about the task at hand, and inspired to drive your traffic to the stars.

On the outside, some of the advice we read about SEO is really helpful, but most of it isn't. If you are a blogger, a content marketer or a writer, you truly need to understand what will work and what really wont and, if you are still waiting for the advice that tells you not to keyword stuff and not to duplicate content then internet marketing is not the job for you; in that case, move on and make way for someone who is really willing to do what it takes to get to the number one spot. We discussed previously about what to look for in a freelancer, and that an understanding of SEO is key – never overlook this point.

The number one secret, the top tip for dominating page one of the search engine results is this – there isn't one.

For those of you that have been looking for that one true tip, the one thing that will whiz you straight to the top, you have been doing nothing more than chasing a dream. You are looking for the next big thing in generating traffic but the real secret to improving your search engine ranking, to driving traffic naturally, is to focus your efforts on people.

It has been made clear on so many occasions, even by Google, that when you take part in online marketing, your focus must not be on you; it must be on the people that you are serving. The blog you are writing is written by you, it isn't about you. You cannot buy whatever product or service it is you are selling, other people have to do that; other people have to read your content and comment on your social media posts, you cannot do that yourself. Every piece of content, every post, every blog must be focused on others. Get to know your audience, and you will be in a much better position to cater to their needs and wants.

Why you are not in the top 10 rank

Be honest, do you really want me to tell you the truth? To tell you why you are not getting anywhere near the top 10 on the search engine ranks? The single biggest reason why so many content writers, so many bloggers, enjoy organic traffic is down to one thing – ignorance.

The second you hear the term "SEO", your mind automatically starts thinking about keyword research, onsite optimization and offsite optimization, anchor links and so many other things that the way ahead is difficult to see. It's all so cloudy that it really isn't possible to see where you are going, and this is what makes you search for shortcuts.

Most people are happy to use a tool to automate a part of their SEO but, in all honesty, that is not really necessary. You can dominate the first page of the search engine ranks without using any tools or without cutting any corners. By reading this book to date, you should see that SEO is certainly not impossible.

Let's take a look at the top 10 secrets to ranking, and to driving organic traffic to your website, without getting bogged down in all the hidden corners of SEO.

1. **Pick one idea and go with it**

You cannot afford to be the jack of all trades that you used to be anymore. It is now time to pick an area and specialize in it, to give it your full focus and address it fully. If the last post you wrote was titled something like "100 ways to start your home business", you need to stop doing that. You need to take just one idea out of that list of 100 and write about it, and write everything you can. The minute you take that one idea, you don't even really need to do too much research on keywords, although you do still need to do some. The best key phrases are going to fall not place without you even trying too hard, and that is the kind of thing that the search engines are looking for.

If you are a content marketer, every single post, every blog, every guest article that you write has to be completely related and relevant to that micro topic you chose. Whatever niche your website is in, the absolute best time to show off your knowledge is right now.

If you are an email marketer, talk about what you know, talk about the best ways to build list, talk about how to write a subject line, about permission marketing and everything else that email marketing entails. Stay focused – that is the number one secret.

2. Answer the "one" question

When you write your content, are you just contributing more noise to the noise that is already out there? Or do you actually answer questions that are relevant?

The only way to stand out in the competitive world of content marketing is to answer relevant questions in your writing. Your target audience is going to have an awful lot of questions that they want answered, but you don't need to answer every single one; find the one question that seems to be bugging the most people and answer that one.

For example, in relation to this, we might have one common question being asked – "what is content marketing?". It is simple, and it is a question that many people ask. When you answer it, provided you answer it properly and naturally, the search engines will pick up on it and send you so much organic traffic you won't know what to do with it all. Additionally, if you are new to the niche that you are writing about then you have a much better chance of hitting the top spot on the search engine ranking pages. Why? You would think that newcomers to the scene would have to work much harder, but keep in mind that your competitors are already established, and they are simply not interested in answering "common" questions any more. It's up to you to take full advantage of this and run with it.

3. Make sure your introduction is rich in keywords

All the time, we read about how important it is to get keywords into your headlines and how to make your headlines clickable. We don't read so much about the introduction to your content, and that part is just as important as the headline.

If you are not using SEO plugins, the introduction to your content will show up on your search engine result, so it is absolutely vital that it is rich in the right keywords for your niche. Those keywords must be natural and they must be relevant. Do not try to stuff keywords into any old place because the search engines will know if they don't read right.

Always start the introduction with your target keyword. The reason for this is that it will give the search engine spiders something to latch on to, something to chow down on. The spider wants to be able to see that what you are writing about is relevant.

If your blog is about content marketing, start your introduction with these words. That is the only way to show the search engine that your content is relevant. Don't stuff keywords in, but make sure you start your introduction with the relevant one, and make them all necessary and natural.

4. **Do watch your spelling and grammar**

This really is a no-brainer. If you are writing a blog or a piece of friendly content, you want to be able to share your experiences, good and bad, with your audience, without sounding like you are standing on a podium, lecturing them. With that in mind, you still have to watch your spelling and your grammar.

Why?

Does it have anything to do with the search engine spiders? Not really. It's all because of your readers. If your work is full of bad grammar and spelling mistakes, people will not come back to you, and they certainly won't put the word around about you. On top of this, other websites will not link to you, and that is one of the most important parts of SEO ranking - having good and relevant links.

The search engines will monitor repeat visits to your website through the use of cookies and cache elements inserted into your browser. If you don't get repeat visitors, it looks bad on you and the search engine will drop your ranking. Therefore, it is important that you do everything you can to get visitors to keep on coming back to you.

Spelling and grammar are fundamental elements and, if you are not so good at them, do one of three things – give it up, take classes, or get someone else to help you write your content. Search engines look closely at the way your readers behave in order to work out how relevant your site is. If your readers stay with you and keep on returning, the search engine knows that you are publishing valuable, relevant content, and with this, they will send you a large amount of unsolicited traffic, traffic that is entirely targeted, and extremely valuable.

5. **Less is the new more**

Really, less is so much better than waffling on. By less, I mean choosing fewer options. Let's assume for a moment that you are speaking to a large room full of people, a room full of beginners to internet marketing. You have to be able to communicate with them at their level, and you have to be able to inspire them to jump into action.

If you were to train them on 30 different ways to get started, it would extremely daunting to them to have to pick the best ones for their situation; instead, you would pick about three to five ways to get them started and watch their conversion rate spiral beyond anything they ever dreamed possible.

In the same way, if you are writing content, do not give it all up in one article or blog post, instead break up your content into bite-sized sections and turn it into a series.

That has two effects – one, you are not boring your readers and, two, they will come back to read the next instalment.

What plays a big role in determine your rankings on the search engines is user experience. Take Google for example; they like their users to be happy because, if they are not, then Google does not get so much money from the AdWords advertisers. The secret here is to make it very easy for your readers to put your tips into practice straightaway, not to have to wade through pages of waffle before they get to the point.

6. Stop chasing, start attracting links

In all honesty, no marketer will ever be 100% happy with the amount of links that they build up manually and, because we have always been told that you need thousands of these links to be successful, many content marketers give up early in the game. They give up because they find it stressful, and too much to continue.

You see, despite the fact that some of these websites have, quite literally, thousands of links, they are still not making it into the top 10 on the search engine ranks. Do you want to know why they cannot get there?

It's simple really.

Instead of attracting the links, they are working too hard at chasing the links. If you write your content well, if you write high quality, relevant content, the links will come to you naturally without you needing to go out on search missions to find them.

Forget link exchanges, they do not work and they are more likely to drop your ranking than raise it. Good quality content, helpful and relevant content, will attract the links. Do not expect people to start linking to your content unless they get some benefit from it. Just write great content, promote it well, then sit back, and count the links from good, authority websites.

7. Use your key term to optimize your images

Another very simple secret that many webmasters neglect to use is to optimize their images. We all know that search engines, Google in particular, now have specific databases for images, but there is a bit of a rule here. If you are working in a very competitive niche, forget using popular keywords – it will not work and you will not get any ranking points for them.

Go down the easy road and optimize your images correctly. If you are targeting a keyword in your headline, use the same one on your image ALT text, in the title and in the description blank spaces. When people look for images, ones that they can use in their own custom designs, graphic designs, web designs, content, and so on, your image will show up, provided it has been optimized properly.

Always use the right images on your content; this way, people will be able to use your image and give your website the real credit as the source. That works to send more traffic your way, thus increasing your potential conversion rate even more.

8. Make your articles at least 1000 words

So many content writers still stick with content of about 500 words, believing that to be the optimum amount. It isn't. 500 words is way too short when you are trying to build up a successful website.

Sure, you can make one or two of them that short but, for the most part stick to writing at least 1000 words per article. Now, I realize that this goes against what I said earlier, about less being more, but that still applies.

In that 1000+ word article, you can still concentrate on just one or two things, but in more detail. Keep the content relevant - keep it high quality but make it longer. With the latest updates to Google, the search engine is now focusing on length as well as relevance and quality.

The one thing you must not do is use padding or fluff to fill out your article, and never, ever copy and paste from somewhere else - that is plagiarism and is highly frowned upon, not to mention opening you up to all sorts of legal trouble.

9. Use Google+ like a pro

Social media marketing is not for everyone but one of the best is Google+, a great place to share content. Google+ is a highly active social networking site and is the one you should be interacting with the most, even more than you do with Facebook, LinkedIn, or Twitter. Share your bet posts and educate everyone who is in your Google+ circle; find solutions to their problems and ask them to leave a comment on your shared posts.

Make sure you use the right keywords to populate your content. This is vital because the Google spider can find it, index it, and push your content to the right people, at the right time.

10. Search, target and then shoot

Almost done, but this is a very important part of dominating that first page on the search engine results. This three-point strategy will work, no matter what niche you are in, and no matter what level you are at.

Think of a large bird of prey, like an eagle - when it is hungry, it searches for prey, just as you search for your target audience. When they find their prey, they target it, the same as you do with your audience. And, when they have targeted the prey, they shoot for it. This is exactly what you do when you locate your optimal audience.

Find your audience, target them with high quality, relevant content, and then shoot, calling them to action.

This is total reiteration on the advice we have given you on how to build a quality website, with a few other SEO related tips thrown in for good measure. Put it all together and you will find traffic coming your way, probably more than you can handle!

Chapter 9

Top 10 SEO Scams and How to Avoid Getting Burned

The term "Search Engine Optimization" is used very widely and, as a result, a large number of so-called SEO experts have appeared out of the woodwork. These "experts" claim to get you guaranteed rankings and make all sorts of promises that are unrealistic, and that they simply cannot deliver on.

These days, you cannot go for long without getting an email or three about SEO or perhaps a call from a self-styled SEO guru who promises to make all of your dreams, in terms of internet marketing, come true. The very best defense that you can use against search engine optimization scams is to educate yourself fully about the subject of SEO.

Most owners of small or startup businesses simply do not have the resources nor the time needed to become experts in the subject so, to help you out, I have come up with a list of the most common scams, the SEO "claims" that you should be aware of.

Please be aware that I am not talking about the claims that are related to paid search results, only the organic, natural results -at the end of the day, anyone can get the top ranking on a paid placement, provided they are prepared to pay the price.

1. **Guaranteed ranking**

A good proportion of SEO claims are centered on the premise of guaranteed rankings. If you see claims such as any of the following, stay away from them:

- Guaranteed number one ranking on Google

- Guaranteed first page ranking on Google

- Guaranteed number one ranking on all search engines

These claims are nigh on impossible to substantiate in terms of organic results. Even Google themselves warn you to steer clear of SEO experts who claim to guarantee your rankings because they say that no one can do that. As it comes direct from the horse's mouth, make sure you stay well away from anyone who makes these claims, or claims like them.

2. **They claim they have contacts at Google**

Totally false. There isn't an SEO expert in the world who can genuinely claim that they know someone at Google, or have a special relationship with the company. If they make this claim, it is a huge red flag that they are lying through their teeth to get your business. Don't be taken in by it.

3. **They offer free trials**

SEO is not an easy job, it is long, tedious and incredibly involved. The process that a true expert will go through to get the result requires a great deal of time and there is no legitimate SEO expert on earth that will offer to do this for free. If, as well as offering you a free trial, they also ask for your FTP username and passwords, or ask for access into your hosting account, think of the damage they could do. If it sounds too good to be true, it most likely is.

4. They offer submissions to thousands of different search engines

More than 95% of the search market on the internet is accounted for through Google, Bing, Yahoo, AOL and MSN. Submissions to thousands of other search engines will gain you absolutely nothing, so concentrate on those that really do matter.

5. Not disclosing or using secret strategies

SEO experts will always tell you exactly what they are going to do to your site to optimize it. They will also be up front about their strategy to build links. If a so-called expert talks about trade secrets, or won't tell you what they are going to do, they are more than likely going to be using black hat techniques. Those techniques are liable to result in a ban from all the major search engines - a total disaster for your business.

6. Top ranking inside of 48 hours

Remember what we talked about? The guarantees of rankings, add to that a deadline, especially one of 48 hours, and you know you are looking at a scam. The only way to achieve the top ranking within 48 hours is by using PPC – Pay Per Click.

7. Lowest price SEO expert

One again, if something sounds too good to be true, it most definitely is. I said earlier that SEO is not easy work and it takes a lot of time to get it right and reap the right results. If an expert claims that he can do it cheaper than anyone else does, do yourself a favor and learn how to do it yourself – you will be better off. The old adage, "you only get what you pay for" is definitely true in this case.

8. They are partners with Google

Or they work with someone at Google. They don't, and they are most definitely not a partner of Google. Google does not have partnerships in the SEO world and no genuine Google employee would put their job on the line by associating, illegally, I might add, with any such company.

9. **They know the algorithm that Google uses**

Or they will claim to be experts in the Google algorithm. Those algorithms are highly complex and are totally dynamic. They may know one or two aspects of it, such as Meta tag, content and link popularity, but they won't now the algorithm that the search engine giant uses. Any expert will know about the important aspects of SEO, so such claims are nothing special.

10. **They want ownership of the content you provide**

If you write the content, or you pay someone else to write that content, it is yours. Ensure that you do not sign any agreement to hand ownership of that content over to anyone else, specifically your SEO agency. A true professional will not ask you to do this. If you do end up handing over ownership, it could be sold on to a competitor for large sums of money and then you will have a job to prove it was yours in the first place.

Chapter 10

The Role of Google Analytics in SEO

There are plenty of tools up for grabs when it comes to SEO, and one of the most popular is Google Analytics. This is a completely free tool that allows you to monitor how visitors are interacting with your website.

When you start your SEO campaign, you should start using Google Analytics straight away, to track the performance of your keywords. You will be able to see how much traffic is brought to your website via each individual keyword and you will also get to know a whole host of information about visitors to your website, which you would never have known otherwise.

Benefits

The following are some of the benefits of using Google Analytics during your SEO campaigns:

1. It's free but still offers up the same level of function, if not higher, than many paid tools do.
2. You can see how visitors are finding your website. Obviously, there is a core keyword set that you are using and optimizing, but Google Analytics will also be able to tell you if visitors are using other keywords that result in your website coming up. When you first start to optimize your website, you

will only use a couple of main keywords but, as time goes by, you can increase these through using Google Analytics and finding out which other keywords are being used the most.

3. You can see which of your pages are visited the most and which links are clicked on the most. Google Analytics will tell you which are the most popular, and it will give you a good idea of whether your campaign is sending people to the right pages.

4. You can see the numbers of new visitors that your SEO campaign is bringing your way, as well as being able to segment your results into referral sources geography and new, or returning visitors.

5. Using the reports from the tool, you will find it easier to fine tune your website. You can see any pages that are not doing so well and concentrate effort on re-writing the content to make it better, and make it convert more. You will be able to gain a lot of new, quality prospects, in this way and potentially, a lot more customers.

Instead of just picking up information about traffic that comes your way from Google, the analytics tool will also allow you to see how much traffic is coming via other search engine, like Yahoo! and MSN. This can help you to determine how strong your hold is on each platform, and you can then strengthen up where necessary.

At the end of the day, each and every marketing campaign must be tracked, whether it's on or offline, to determine how well it is doing. You need to know where the problems are to be able to fix them and you can only do that by using tools like Google Analytics.

5 Google Analytic strategies to measure your SEO success

There is an old saying in the world of SEO – "if you can't measure it, you can't improve it". When it comes to SEO, measurement is the most critical factor in success.

While keyword rankings are a very good measure for SEO, and they can be responsible for a high level of traffic to your website, using keywords alone can seriously devalue your role as a marketer, and it doesn't give you a full picture as to why SEO is so important to you.

Getting beyond the rankings for keywords will allow you and your marketing team to showcase what is really important – how organic searches bring real profit and plenty of revenue, not to mention value, to your business. Google Analytics is a vital tool for measuring the success of your website and, if you are not using it now, you should be.

While each business is unique and will have its own set of metrics to look at and measure success by, the following 5 ways to make use of Google Analytics will benefit you, no matter what niche you are in.

1. **How to see organic search traffic only**
This might be somewhat obvious to some people, and it is quite surprising how many businesses register a drop in website traffic and immediately blame it on a decline in traffic from organic searches. Sometimes, just digging a little deeper below the surface can show you that organic search traffic is on the rise, whilst other sources are down, and that is where the overall decline comes in.

To use Google Analytics to look at your organic search traffic, click on **Acquisition.** Then select **All Traffic,** followed by **Channels,** and then click on **Channel Grouping.** You will now see your website traffic split into channels.

If you click on **Organic Search Channel** you will see a detailed report that shows you the metrics just for organic searches - this report is absolutely vital to your SEO campaign. From here, you can see which of your pages are the top landing spots for search traffic, the keywords that drive the most traffic your way, which search engines send the most traffic to you, which pages are the top exit pages, and so much more besides.

2. How to measure SEO traffic quality

Many times, you will hear it said that you can't measure quality because it is subjective - this simply is not true, and there are many ways to measure the quality of your traffic sources, not just the search sources.

The most common and perhaps the best report you can use to measure if there are any improvements or declines in search traffic quality, is called the **Assisted Conversions** report. To access this, click on **Conversions,** followed by **Multi-Channel Funnels,** and then click on **Assisted Conversions.**

Start off by setting your date range to "**Last Month**" and then compare it with **"Previous Period".** What you will see is a comparison, on a month to month basis, of conversions that come straight from a search, or, where there are several visits to the site, conversions in which search played a part, but cannot be directly attributed to the conversion. An example of this would be a person that found your company via a search term but then came back to the site directly and converted, without going through the search engine again.

This report will show you if there are any drops or improvements in conversions that come from search traffic. If you spot a decline, even though overall search traffic is holding steady, you will be able to see that the search traffic is either not qualified or it is of a low quality. By the same measure, if you focus on a refined keyword set and you can see a big improvement in search traffic conversions, you will now that your quality of traffic is definitely improving.

3. Assigning a financial value to organic traffic

This is a good strategy for those businesses who want to understand what value is being brought to their business by SEO, beyond the normal traffic improvements, conversions, and visibility. We do this by assigning a value to the organic traffic results.

To do this, you need to compare the cost of the keywords if they were purchased though a Google AdWords campaign. You will need to have a Google AdWords account for this to work, and your Google Analytics account must be synced with your Search Console account.

To find the keyword search phrases and queries for your website, open **Acquisition,** followed by **Search Engine Optimization,** and then **Queries.**

When you open this report, you should then open up your AdWords account in another page. In AdWords click on **Tools,** followed by **Keyword Planner,** and then choose the option that says **Get Search Volume Data and Trends.** Type in the top keywords which are in your Google Analytics Queries and click on **Get Search Volume.** Another screen will appear, click on **Keyword Ideas.**

Each of the keywords you input will come up with a suggested bid amount, an estimate of what advertisers are paying for every click on the keyword.

Open up a spreadsheet and list down all of the keywords that drive traffic to your website, the number of clicks for each one, and the estimated CPC – cost per click. The last column in your spreadsheet will be the total of the estimated CPC multiplied by the number of clicks, and that gives you the organic traffic value.

This is a good strategy to use when you want an idea of what your SEO strategy is, saving you on traffic that you would have had to pay for.

4. **How to identify slow page loading times**
One of the metrics that is overlooked time and time again by SEO experts is page loading time, and the need to

optimize it. Page speed is now a major page ranking factor as well as being something that affects how a user experiences your website. If you are spending money and investing time in keyword rankings and SEO, don't throw it all away by ignoring a website that is slow to load up.

What I am not going to do is tell you how to make your website load faster; instead, we are going to look at how you identify which pages are slow at loading, and how to measure the impact that has on your conversion rates.

To measure this on an individual page basis, open up **Behavior,** followed by **Site Speed,** and then **Page Timings**. Set the middle column to **"Average Page Load Time"** and then set the right column to **"% Exit"**. You can also set **Secondary Dimension** to **Medium,** and set the filter so it only shows organic traffic.

This report will show you the average time that each page takes to load fully and the average number of visitors who exit on the page. It should be fairly easy to see that, as your page load time gets longer, the number of exits will also begin to rise.

As an SEO marketer, you would need to go to the developers of the site and ask them to take a look at how they can optimize the speed. Once the loading times are better, run the report again and compare it with the first one. This will show you if you have managed to retain additional search traffic and the number of conversions

5. **Create your own dashboard**

Sometimes, to get someone to move from being a sceptic to a believer in what you do, it takes nothing more than the way in which the data is presented. Internet marketers or SEO experts, tend to over-explain everything or come out with metrics that are not easy for everyone to grasp. At times, all the client wants is a simple pie chart or bar graph, not over-complicated explanations and terms they have never heard of before, and probably never want to hear again.

The best way to do this is to use the dashboard interface built in to Google Analytics. The dashboard is nothing more than a number of widgets that bring all of the individual reports into one, easy to access view, a view that can be shared and printed as well. The big bonus here is that using this dashboard properly will also reduce the amount of time you spend looking at the analytics, which leaves you more free time to concentrate on the actual SEO.

To create your own dashboard, click on **Dashboard,** followed by **+ New Dashboard.** The first widget to set up is a counter that measures the total number of visits to your website from organic searches. To do this, click on **Add Widget** and then call it **Total Organic Visits.** Stick with the Metric display for now, you can always change it later.

Click on **Show the Following Metric**, then choose **Sessions.** Because you only want the organic search visits counted you must now create a filter. Click on **Filter this Data**, click on **Only Show**, followed by **Medium**, then **Exactly Matching,** and finally, click on **Organic.**

One more widget to set up is one that measures your keyword phrases, sorted by the number of sessions and the goal completions that result from each keyword. Add your widget as you did earlier, but this time click on **Display the Following Columns,** and choose **Keyword,** followed by **Sessions,** and then **Goal Completions**. You want the display set as a **Table**. Use the instructions above to set the same organic filter to this widget.

You can tailor these reports how you want them, but you should include the following metrics:

- All organic visits over time (Timeline)

- Top SEO landing pages
- Top organic keywords & % of new visits
- Pages per visit by organic keyword
- Most successful keywords by goal completions

Turn a Challenge into a Strength

The most challenging part of SEO is the ability to effectively determine the value that you are bringing to the business by your efforts. It is very easy for you to show or tell another SEO how the numbers are improving, but try explaining it to someone who isn't in the know and you will stumble and fall.

You must be able to quantify your work from the standpoint of traffic and revenue, to be able to show that you are bringing in and retaining new business. If the person who hired you doesn't understand what you are telling them, it won't be long before they move on.

Pay close attention to the metrics that your clients want and find a good way of including this in your SEO reports. If your client or manager has shared access to the analytics, be sure to walk through with them how to use it; tell them exactly what you are using and why, tell them what the widgets are tracking and why the numbers are important, use simple language, and then, and only then, will they learn to appreciate how much value you bring to the business.

Chapter 11

AdWords or SEO -Which One Should You Use?

Two of the biggest components in SEM – Search Engine Marketing – are SEO and AdWords. They are two of your most valuable tools, especially in a digital marketing campaign. They have their differences and they have their similarities, but there are certain situations where you will need to decide which to use, or whether to use them together.

If you are a new entrant to the world of digital marketing, you will already have heard mention of things like PPC (Pay Per Click) and AdWords. You will have heard of CPC (cost per click) campaigns and bids, but you may not be entirely sure what it is all about.

AdWords is Google's own advertising platform, a platform that advertisers use to get their ads in the search page results, in YouTube, Gmail and other Google Products, as well as to the hundreds of thousands of websites that take part in AdSense.

If you are an advertiser, you can opt between paying for each click on your advert (CPC), or for when people actually see your ad (CPM – cost per thousand impressions). In short, AdWords is very much like a huge auction site where advertisers are in competition against one another for the best advertising spots.

AdWords vs SEO

Now that you know what AdWords is, and you already know what SEO is, let's look at how they compare with one another:

- AdWords is only for websites that use AdSense and for Google websites, while SEO is applicable to every single search engine.
- AdWords traffic is most definitely paid for while SEO traffic is sometimes free
- AdWords ads show up on the top and at the side of the Google Search; in some situations, you can get your hands on one, while SEO involves a lot more work to get to one of those top spots.
- AdWords is far quicker than SEO; the effects are almost immediate because you can come up with an ad campaign pretty much straight away, getting your targeted traffic quickly. SEO, on the other hand, takes time, especially if your website is new, to get good page rankings and a decent amount of traffic.
- With AdWords you can calculate your ROI (Return on Investment) much easier, while SEO contains a lot more factors that make it harder, not just spend and revenue.
- When you halt your AdWords campaign, traffic to your website will also stop, but with SEO, once you are getting organic traffic, it will continue to flow.
- AdWords allows you to target large numbers of keywords at the same time, but with SEO you have to pick just a few of the best to get the best result.
- AdWords allows you to advertise on Google websites and those that use AdSense, while SEO results can only come from the search engines.

Which one should you use?

As a new company, your best bet is to start with AdWords, because it is the quickest way to get traffic to your website. SEO takes time to achieve this while, with AdWords, it is almost instantaneous. However, you will find it quite expensive to start with, but, if your campaigns are showing signs of real profit, you can justify the expenditure, and you can meet your objectives.

New companies want to get traffic quickly because they want to make quick sales, they want to find new customers quickly, and they also want their website tested out, with their products and all the other parts of their sales and marketing process.

Provided you use AdWords properly and carefully, you will find success. However, it is incredibly easy to spend money with abandon on AdWords and, if you don't have the right tools in place to monitor it, you will end up spending far more than you make. The system has been made simple to use but, if you are not experienced or have insufficient knowledge, keep your money in the bank and either hire someone else to do it for you, or choose to go down the SEO route.

If you do choose to get started with AdWords, you also need to run an SEO campaign at the same time, as well as content and social media marketing. Used together, these three tools are everything you need for success online for the long term.

Content marketing will help you to get the right content out there; SEO helps to get that content optimized for the search engines, and social media helps to promote your newly optimized content to a much bigger audience.

Using SEO and AdWords together

There are those who say that, when you are getting a nice steady stream of traffic via SESO, there is no need to use AdWords - wrong.

Even if your rankings are good, AdWords still has a part to play in giving you more exposure on those SEO keywords. AdWords campaigns are measurable and, if you find that you are pulling in a profit, you can easily increase your budget for even more return on your investment.

To make the most out of your marketing campaign, you should use both SEO and AdWords together. Use AdWords to start the traffic rolling and, at the same time, work on your SEO, content and social media plans to bring the traffic in from other directions. At the end of the day, AdWords works well in the short term, while SEO is best used for long term results.

Chapter 12

The Role of Webmaster in SEO

Google offers up a number of useful tools for you to use in your SEO campaign, and while Google Analytic is the most obvious one, Webmaster is a close second.

Google Webmaster is designed for advanced search experts, to give them another perspective on evaluating and planning their search efforts. Here's an overview on how to use Google Webmaster to further your SEO campaign.

Google Webmaster background

Webmaster is vital for the success of any strong SEO campaign. To understand how to use these tools to their full advantage, you need to have an understanding of the role they play, in seeing your website exactly as Google sees it. The tools give you a number of different insights, including telling you which of your pages have been popular, the links that point to your website, the most popular keyword on your website, and much more besides.

A website that is active in Google Webmaster has a much better chance of being indexed fully and of ranking very well, and that's without the deeper insights that you can use to run your SEO campaign into tactical gold. If you have not yet set up your website on Google webmaster, it is easy to get started – simply sign up for your account and then log in to the Webmaster dashboard, where you can add your website.

First, you will need to verify that your domain is owned by you and, depending on which host you are using, you might be given access to verification via a pop-up process, which allows you to log in and to verify the domain in a couple of steps.

Some of the other options for verification include uploading an HTML file to the root folder on your site, inputting a metatag provided by Google on your homepage, or confirming that you own the domain through Google Analytics, provided it is installed on your website. Once you have completed the verification, data will begin populating within 24 to 48 hours.

Google Webmaster features to use

When your website is set up on Webmaster, you can log in and explore the interface, get to know your way around, and find out what is available. At its very core, Webmaster is all about the important metrics – what gets linked, what get indexed, and where the traffic is going. If you can break all that data down into ways that make sense to you, and look at it with a view to learning certain things, you will get more out of the information. From all of this data you can easily come up with a plan about where your campaign needs to head.

Search Queries

Search Queries give you information on keywords and traffic. Whilst you could easily go and look at Google Analytic for this information, Webmaster gives you a different perspective on the same information. It won't just give you a breakdown of all the traffic that found its way to your website; instead, it will give you impressions that show what your traffic potential is, and your site ranking across the Google search results. Search Queries is split into five main areas:

- **Query** - Provides you with details on which keywords your website is currently ranking for. This is a fast way to find out if your efforts in respect of a particular keyword are actually working or not. Do keep in mind that the term "rank for" means that it shows up in the SERPs – Search Engine Results Page, but isn't necessarily attracting the traffic just yet. The Query feature can help you to determine which keywords are relevant but need a bit of a kick from further optimization or linking.

- **Impressions** – Do you ever wonder how many people visit your website from a specific keyword search? Impressions will tell you the answer. This one will give you an overall idea of how many people see certain sections of your website content and it will also help you to confirm how valuable a keyword is, as well as the data that comes from the Google Keywords Module.

- **Clicks** – OK, so let's say 100,000 people have seen your website; how many of those are actually clicking on your website? Clicks will tell you how many people actually click on the search result to go to your site.

- **CTR** – Click through rate is the percentage of those who click on the search result, who actually to go to your website. If your rates are looking a little on the low side, you should take a look at whether your page meta description should be updated or changed. Ask yourself if the content could be more relevant to the queries that drive the highest number of impressions on that page. Consider the broader search landscape at the same time – is PPC activity actually sending traffic away from your branded results?

- **Average Position** – This one tells you where your website is ranking for each of your keywords. Overall, the most traffic will head towards the websites in the top 2 or 3 positions for any given search term, so you want to know how you perform against those positions, and what the impact is on your traffic.

Monitoring trends over time

If you have just launched a brand new SEO strategy and you want to know how effective it is, use the "**With Change**" feature in Webmaster. This will change the perspective and give you your current stats, as well as looking at how your performance changes over time.

You can use this data in a couple of ways. For example, if you have recently changed the content on your site, this tool can show whether your changes are effective or not. You can also use it to see if your average conversions and rankings have been affected by any Google Updates. Tracking this information over a period of time is the best way to monitor what is going on, and to keep your SEO strategy up to date with the current landscape, in terms of SEO.

Individual keywords

If you want to know how a particular keyword is performing, while you are in the Search Query area, click on the keyword. If you look deeper into the data for each of your keywords, you will get a better idea regarding how your pages rank for each keyword. This will also help you gain a better understanding of your SEO success overall and it will also tell you if the content you develop is effective enough at targeting those keywords. On top of this, you will also see any connections between target and existing content, connections you may not have seen before now.

Use top pages to find opportunity

Inside the Search Query area, you will be able to see your Top Pages - this is where you find out which content is gaining the most impressions and clicks, and is also where you can find opportunities that you can capitalize on.

For example, if you have a piece of content that is getting a really good click through rate but is only ranking on page 2 of SERPs, you could consider building links to the page to try and get it on page 1. The real key is in understanding that your audience may be focused on something you didn't expect, and finding out what they are focusing on will help you to change your strategy, and to take advantage of it.

Refining page level strategy

When you built your website, you most likely picked targeted keywords for each page or content sections; Webmaster lets you reverse that process and identify which keyword each page is ranking for. The results will almost certainly contain the keywords you chose, but there may be a few surprises in there as well.

Once you have worked out the keywords on each page, add them in to a tool for rank tracking and you will get some extra data to use in your strategy, such as competition and traffic. This will help you to find opportunities that have not yet been exploited.

Make sure that your pages contain all the keywords they rank for, especially in page titles and the first paragraph of the content.

Chapter 13

How to Use SEO for Website Promotion

Traffic is the life of your website, so it makes sense that you increase traffic to it by way of promoting your website.

Website promotion should be an integral part of any SEO strategy and it should be the logical next step after you have done all your optimization, to make your website perform as you want it to in the search engines. For example, site promotion can be a great help in improving your ranking in the search engines, and in getting your website to move a lot quicker.

Why does my website need to be promoted?

Because it is the easiest way to get more traffic flowing to your website.

Think of site promotion in terms of advertising your products and services, but much cheaper, if not free. Site promotion is a big part of SEO and it means using keywords that the search engines pick up on, and to help people find you. It also involves using social media to gain a following, and potential new customers, as well as having your site listed on local directories.

The internet can reach much further than traditional forms of advertising and it is also so much easier to measure your success. There are lots of ways you can use to get noticed, so jump in and do it.

How to promote your website

- Use a campaign creation tool that lets you target your advertising by using your keywords, and then only paying when your link is clicked.
- Get your website on the search engines – there are three major ones that you should concentrate on – Google, Bing and Yahoo! The first page to submit is your sitemap because this will allow the search engines to pick up on any changes to your website, without you having to tell them whenever you add or take something away. By submitting your website to the search engines, you are telling them that you are there, and you are telling them which pages are on your website.
- Get your website listed in the local directories and the online ones. There are tons of article directories to be found on the web, and most of them will accept unpaid article submissions to their databases. What you should do is come up with some highly informative articles that are related to your niche or industry, and then submit them to the directories. Make sure you include an Author Bio at the end of the article, with a link to your website. When you ask for your articles to be included in a directory, you are actually giving everyone permission to reprint that article on a website, in a newsletter, on a blog, or in any other internet publication, so long as the Author Bio is left intact and a link to your website, that means your articles get more widely published, and more people should come and visit your website. In addition to this, you will get more links back as well.

- Carry out some off-page optimization. Whilst you are busy marketing, don't forget the offline marketing side of things, such as flyers, business cards, and physical adverts. No matter what you do, make sure that your website is included on everything, along with your social networking pages as well. Everything you can do to get your name out there off-line will increase what happens online. As we all know, more quality traffic to websites means higher rankings, and higher rankings mean more traffic. It's an effective circle that just keeps on going, and keeps on building.

- Keep on coming up with new content. One of the most important parts to any optimization strategy is the regular addition of more content, especially up to date and relevant content. By doing this, you are giving your visitors a good reason to visit your site, and you are also giving the search engines a good reason to come back to you as well. The search engines want to be able to give searchers the most up to date version of each website they index, and they also want to add new or improved information as well. The type of content you produce is entirely down to you, and your business requirements. You can add a blog post, run some kind of promotion, upload videos or images, and so much more. You should also publish your updated website to your social media sites as this will also increase your visibility, and attract a wider range of people.

- Get linking. Link building is one of the most important parts of any SEO strategy, provided you do it right. Search engines are hitting up on links and they will examine every link that comes to your site, as well as the ones that go away from your site. They will also look at the status of each one, to see how much traffic they get, and to see if they are genuine links. Search engines do tend to be more favorable towards sites that do not have reciprocal links, and it is a good way to get started. The best thing to do is look for websites in the same niche or topic as yours and contact the webmaster to see if they want to do a link exchange with you. You can also contact your local Visitors Bureau or Chamber of Commerce, to see if link exchanges are possible. Speak to your family, to your friends, and all your social networking contacts, to see if they want to exchange links as well.

- Use those keywords properly. It's no good just picking a keyword because it sounds good; you have to do your research and you have to find the keywords that are the best for your niche Then you have to use them right – in your content, in your page titles, your meta tags, meta descriptions, all the places that the search engines look at, so they can provide the right results for search terms.

- Use social media to promote your site to a wider audience. This is one of the best ways to develop a potentially huge following for your website. Being active on social media sites will drive a lot of traffic to your site, as well as the opportunity to develop a large number of relevant back links. The idea behind this is to get social, and put a human face on your business, whilst still promoting your website and your business. Make sure that you add widgets to your website, especially widgets for all the social networking sites that your business is active on. This will allow visitors to your site to easily share your content with their friends or followers, and that is another way to increase your audience and drive traffic to your website.

- Get a blog up and running. Writing a blog is a fantastic way to keep your website up to date with the most relevant and regular content. If you don't want to add one to your existing website, you can always start a separate blog site, and, if you use WordPress, you won't need to pay for it.

Chapter 14

Tips for Optimizing Your SEO Strategy

No matter what type of marketing campaign you are working on, search engine optimization is the pivotal point in the success or otherwise of your plan. Unfortunately, the search engines are constantly making changes to their search algorithms, so how on earth are you meant to be able to keep up with it all?

The following advice and tips come from seasoned professionals, and are designed to help you find your way around SEO as the search engines constantly evolve. Make sure you are truly set up for SEO success by understanding the following points.

1. **Document your strategy**
As soon as you have finished reading this, get set and write your plan down. Your SEO strategy has to be documented, every single step. Start with a basic strategy and monitor it, then, when you have done some work on analyzing the results of your efforts, you can make the relevant changes. Having it all down in writing is absolutely vital for success; you can't possibly follow a plan without having it all laid out. SEO strategists who have their plan well documented are twice as likely to see success, compared to those who don't.

2. **Your SEO campaign and content marketing campaign are partners, not opponents.**

No doubt you already know of the so-called debate between SEO and content marketing, and I did touch on the differences earlier. There are agencies that specialize in one or the other, and they benefit from widening the gap between the two, however, this can be very damaging to your plan, and the success of your strategy. Content marketing and SEO are not in competition with one another. If you are coming up with content that supports your marketing goals and objectives, it should be fully optimized to increase the potential for your content to be located via the search engines. So, stop messing about and wasting time thinking about whether to opt for SEO or content marketing, use the two together and reap the rewards, whilst watching those who shun one in favor of the other fall at the first hurdle.

3. **Make sure you audit your SEO progress**

One of the first steps you need to take to improve your strategy is to audit your progress on your current SEO strategy. With the search engine algorithms changing on an ever increasing basis, it is vital that you consistently and regularly re-evaluate your plan. This is the only way you can possibly keep up with all the changes and continue moving forward - checking on your current progress is the only way to know where the improvements need to be made.

4. **Think about the "4 Vs" of semantic search**

Search is a personalized thing and that means that the traditional metrics of keyword and page ranking are no longer all that meaningful in terms of measuring SEO success. Searches are becoming more and more focused on semantics, or search context, and marketers have to change the way they evaluate their success. There are four components to semantic searches – volume, variety, velocity, and veracity and all of these should be incorporated into how you target your efforts, as well as how you promote them and measure your success.

A semantic search is a term that is often used instead of "contextual search", and it means "how the search engine discerns the context and the user intent, so that it can return definitive answers, instead of the usual hierarchical list of guesses that used to be presented." Confused? Put simply, semantic search helps the search engine to give the user better results.

When the search engine considers user intent, it means that two people who input the same search terms could get different results. These results are impacted by the location of the user, their search history, their social media networks, and so on, depending on the algorithm used by that particular search engine.

As well as considering user intent context, the search engines also try to incorporate the context of the content into the results as well. This means that search engines are moving away from keyword-driven searches, and are using meta data, like rich snippets, synonyms, and other information available on the site or page of the result, to determine whether a result is relevant to the user.

Finally, in terms of better results, search engines are returning results that are relevant and useful. Instead of just giving searchers a list of results, the search engines are trying to anticipate their needs and give them answers.

5. Use the right keywords

Although searches are heading towards being more context-driven, it is still important that you choose the right keywords, and use them in the right way. If you produce content for the Internet without thinking about keywords and search engine optimization, you will still rank for something, but you run a big risk of failing on your SEO strategy. Make sure that you research your keywords and use them properly, to gain the best results.

6. Optimize all of your content

As soon as you have your target keywords, you need to make sure that your content is fully optimized for them. Use keywords in the right concentration, and in the right places. The most important things to remember are to use your highest ranking keywords in your meta description, your content title, the first paragraph and the last paragraph of your content, and you must also ensure that your keywords are used in a natural way - not inserted into your content any old how. Your readers do not want to see content that looks or reads like spam.

7. Include SEO in your social media efforts

If you truly want to succeed in the world of sematic search, you have to make sure your social media efforts and your SEO efforts complement each other. That way, you are experiencing the best of both worlds and driving more, high quality visitors to your website.

8. Make sure you use the right SEO agency

Should you choose to go down the route of hiring a professional agency, you must make sure you choose the right one. You do not want one that sees SEO and social media marketing as polar opposites, nor one that separates content marketing out from the rest either. Instead, you want an agency who will use all of these strategies together, each complementing the other. Using an agency that favors one means a high possibility of ruining your chances of success.

9. Take full advantage of the SEO power of outside websites

One of the biggest parts of SEO success are inbound links from paid, earned, and owned media. One of the biggest successes in terms of outside sites comes from a website called Slide Share - one you have no doubt heard of.

Slide Share is search friendly, and that means when you post content on it, it is very likely to rank high on the Google SERPS. Any presentation that is posted on Slide Share is translated automatically to text, meaning search engines can find it easier than if the same content was on your own website. Use sites like Slide Share to leverage the power of your own SEO strategy, and to take your results to another level.

10. **Make use of rich snippets**

Rich snippets are a very powerful SEO tactic. They are a way of marketing your content in a way that lets the search engines enhance the results they display. There are lots of different types of rich snippet, including video previews, ratings, and images. The data makes the content far more appealing to the search engine and it can help you to get more clicks from the searchers, when it is displayed alongside the search listing. In short, they can make your content look much more enticing and more engaging to a searcher than a standard listing.

11. **Don't forget to measure your success**

When you no longer have just one set home page, it can be a little difficult to measure your success. However, there are several ways that you can gauge the success of your SEO strategy, as it ties to your content marketing strategy. One of the very best ways to do this is to use a tool like Google Analytics. This allows you to measure the true success of both your SEO strategy and your content marketing strategy, using different metrics to learn new things about your business, and see where any improvements need to be made.

12. **Use SEO to improve all of your content marketing**

While the constant changes in SEO and search engine algorithms can be somewhat frustrating, you should be happy about one thing - the wealth of data that is produced by your SEO strategy can be easily used to improve on your other marketing strategies. Using the free tools available, such as Google Analytics and Google Webmaster, you can build up a specific picture of how your overall strategy is working, and then apply the same to your other strategies. Don't forget to tie your content marketing and SEO strategies together for a boost in success.

Perhaps the most important step is that you should never stop learning about the power of SEO and how to do it properly; because SEO is ever-changing, there is always new information and new data coming out on a regular basis, which can help you to refine your strategy and improve your results.

How much revenue should you put towards your SEO needs?

We have talked at length about how important SEO is, whether you decide to do it yourself or you pay someone else to do the honors for you, but we know that money is not an endless pot; if your particular pot is endless, then you're very lucky indeed!

How much cash you should drive into your SEO strategy is a personal decision but you need to look at it sensibly. Yes, you need traffic to bring you business, in order for your company to survive, so that says that you need to be spending some cash on your SEO needs, but you shouldn't be overdoing it either.

Here are a few ways you can cut costs but still reap the plentiful rewards of SEO:

Basically do it yourself. If you're going to do this, make sure you know what you're doing. Research, read books, ask around for people to show you things, find someone you can trust who does their own SEO and ask for a few handy tips. This isn't something you can go into half-heartedly, so if you're going to do it DIY, make sure you can actually put the time and skills into the job. Look at it this way – if you were going to wallpaper your living room, you wouldn't simply buy what you think you need and soldier on hoping for the best, would you? Well, think of your SEO requirements as the same. Preparation and research is key.

Use more organic SEO methods than paid methods. This is probably the biggest money saver you will find, however it's worth noting that paid SEO is certainly something you should be taking advantage of to some degree. Look at your overall budget and set perhaps one quarter of it aside for paid SEO, such as AdWords, and make more use of free methods if your cash-flow is a little on the shorter side. It might sound like a total contradiction after you read the many paid SEO methods in this book, and why they are so important and effective, but at the same time, it's no good bankrupting yourself if you can't afford it. Be realistic – organic SEO is very effective too, and probably more authentic in many ways.

Write your own content. Using a freelancer is a great way to get quality content onto your website, because you're basically making use of someone else's talents, however if you can't afford to pay a freelancer, you're going to have to do it yourself. Not everyone is a writer, and it's not something that is particular easy, however having said that, it's not impossible either. Any content you write must be perfect in terms of language, spelling, and grammar, up to date, useful, relevant, realistic, creative, and attention grabbing. If you can tick all of those boxes, then you don't need to pay someone else to do it for you.

Manage your own website. If you don't know how to set up a website, by all means pay someone else to do the ground work for you, because the basics are something you need to get right, however once that is done, learn how to manage the site yourself, without having to pay someone else to do it for you. Again, read books, go on a course, research on the Internet, but arm yourself with the skills to do the job yourself, for free.

Remember that you do need to pour some cash into your SEO strategy, because it literally is the difference between success and failure. Having said that, you don't need to throw an awful lot of cash at it, because if you get it right, SEO will work for you, without major need to work too hard, to spend too much cash.

Think of it this way – if you spend too much money on your SEO needs, it's basically false economy, because anything you do make is going to end up backfilling the cost of your efforts!

Conclusion

I would like to thank you for taking the time to download and read my book. I hope that you found it useful.

SEO is not a walk in the park, and so many people get it wrong; the main reason for this is that they do not know what they are doing. So many businesses make the rookie mistake of trying to do everything, of trying to fit every SEO method they can think of into their plan, and this is a fast track to failure.

Start small; pick one or two methods and use them. Monitor how well, or not, they are doing, and if they work, leave them in place; if they don't work, cut your losses and try something else. Don't quit on a method after a day or two though; you should wait at least a couple of weeks, if not a month, before you start to assess the impact it has had on your business.

If you really do not know what you are doing with SEO then do not try to muddle through – this can do a serious amount of damage to your business. Find the money to hire a professional SEO expert to help you out. It may be an outlay you cannot justify at the start but, when you see the results and the money flooding in, you will see that it was a good investment.

Once again, thank you for downloading my book. If you found it helpful, please take a few minutes to leave a review for me at Amazon.com.

CPSIA information can be obtained at www.ICGtesting.com
Printed in the USA
LVOW10s1329130916

504423LV00021B/456/P